Am I Done Yet?

A Comprehensive Guide
to
Retirement

David Magnuson, Esq., CFP®

This book is intended to serve as a guide to help you navigate the challenging process of planning for retirement. It is not a substitute for personalized advice from a financial planner.

Shipwright Press

Manufactured in the United States of America

Library of Congress Cataloging-in-Publication Data
Am I Done Yet? : A Comprehensive Guide to Retirement /
David Magnuson
p. cm.
Includes index.

1. Retirement income–Planning. 2. Retirees, Finance, Personal. 3. Investments. 4. Finance, Personal

ISBN 978-0-9829353-4-7 Paperback

ISBN 978-0-9829353-3-0 Hardcover

CONTENTS

Am I Done Yet?

A Comprehensive Guide
to
Retirement

INTRODUCTION

The Challenge

"Retirement" is a loaded term that spans a broad array of aspirations and concerns. The thought of retiring may conjure up images of sailing across the South Pacific in a sparkling new catamaran, a glass of champagne in hand and snorkeling gear at the ready, attending a gala in support of the vibrant art community in a bustling metropolis, snuggling with the grandkids on the front porch of a quaint farmhouse, attending classes at the local university, or living in a double-wide, yelling at the television in outrage over the latest political gaffe of that other party. Well, maybe not the latter, but retirement certainly means different things to different people.

The uncomfortable truth is that a majority of Americans aren't confident in their ability to retire. Private sector pensions, once the pillar of many retirement plans, have all but disappeared in the face of cost-cutting measures intended to enhance the profitability of businesses. As private sector pensions fade away, defined contribution plans such as 401(k)s shift the responsibility of accumulating retirement funds to employees. Sadly, this experiment has failed the average American. Vanguard indicates that the median 401(k) account balance at the end of 2020 was a paltry $33,472. Given this unsettling fact, perhaps it is not surprising that only 12 percent of employees who participate in 401(k)s contribute the maximum allowable annual amount. The sobering statistics go on and on, and the message is clear—a retirement crisis is brewing in the United States.

I wrote this book because I am passionate about helping individuals navigate the many challenges associated with retirement.

I want you to take your place in the upper quartile of Americans who are confident in their ability to retire, and to reach this goal, I want you to begin planning now. This book is intended to help you determine (a) whether you should retire, (b) whether you can retire, and (c) how you can accomplish this surprisingly challenging financial maneuver.

As a wealth manager, I've spent countless hours counseling clients on the fundamentals of retirement planning, and this book is my attempt to package what I know into a manageable primer. Nearly every topic I address in this book is the subject of a dissertation published in a peer-reviewed journal by an exceptionally intelligent specialist with an exceptionally large capacity for minutiae. And while I personally enjoy "geeking out" on this stuff (to use the parlance of my teenage daughter), my assumption is that you don't. While you may be able to recite the Iliad in Ancient Greek or rebuild an aircraft engine while blindfolded, my assumption is that you'd rather spend your time in retirement doing anything other than debating whether the efficient market devotees or behavioralists have a better grasp of the fundamentals of investing.

How to Use This Book

Retirement is a complex topic, and when I put pen to paper and started drafting this book, I quickly recognized that focusing solely on the financial elements of retirement planning would be a disservice to readers. The critical question of whether you *should* retire also merits careful consideration and marks the beginning of our journey together. This largely therapeutic analysis is followed by a financial reality-check and then a series of chapters that explore the fundamentals of accumulating assets sensibly, creating income effectively, and organizing your estate. This is how the chapters of this book work together:

Chapter 1: *Should I?*

The first chapter asks you to contemplate whether retiring is advisable, even if immediately handing in your thirty-day notice is a possibility. If your answer is a clear yes, proceed to Chapter 2 without delay. If your answer is no, digesting the rest of this book is still important, but you can take your time.

Chapter 2: *Can I?*

This chapter is your reality-check. By the end of the analysis, you should have a better sense of whether your existing assets are sufficient to carry you through your retirement years.

Chapter 3: *How? (Part I: Investing Intelligently)*

Whether you are on the verge of retirement or many years of wealth accumulation lie ahead, this chapter will help you come up with a sound investment plan.

Chapter 4: *How? (Part II: Creating Stable Retirement Income)*

Creating a steady stream of income in retirement in a tax-effective manner merits careful analysis. This chapter helps you create a sensible plan for meeting your cash-flow needs.

Chapter 5: *Other Assets*

This chapter explores asset classes other than cash, stocks, and bonds, such as real estate, gold, annuities, and life insurance.

Chapter 6: *Legacy Planning*

The oft-neglected topic of establishing an organized and effective estate plan is the topic of the final chapter of this book.

CHAPTER 1

Should I?

The title of this chapter presupposes that you have a choice when it comes to retiring. Maybe you don't. In my wealth management practice, I routinely encounter clients who have been forced out of their jobs due to rampant age discrimination in the tech world. As technology continues to evolve and skillsets quickly become obsolete, new talent is routinely brought into the labor force at the expense of older, more costly employees. If this describes you, I apologize for the very title of this book. *Am I Done Yet?* could more appropriate be re-titled, *I Guess I'm Done.*

This sad phenomenon of forcing older tech workers out of the labor force prematurely aside, I often work with clients who are doing quite well, and while they can clearly retire early, they aren't sure if they should. I must confess that I had a not-so-secret weapon in writing this chapter. My wife, Janelle, happens to be a very good Marriage and Family Therapist who helps clients grapple with this issue. This chapter is the result of hours of back-and-forth between the two of us, as well as considerable research on the critical topic of happiness in our golden years.

What Brings You Joy?

The study of happiness is a burgeoning field in psychology. It's about time. Whoever said that life had to be a dreary march toward a gold wristwatch and days spent watching reruns of *Friends?* When deciding whether retiring is the right choice for you, I want you to think hard about what makes you happy. Better yet, you'll note that I use the word joy in the title of this section. This is intentional. Happiness is nice. Joy is nicer. It is unrestrained and powerful, and yet connotes a certain vulnerability that can only come with a true sense of self. For much of this chapter, I will try to get you to think about what brings you joy, and whether you are well-prepared for a joyful retirement.

Work?

One of my favorite movies is *October Sky*, the true story of an insatiably driven and curious teenager who breaks free of a gritty West Virginia coal-mining town by winning the National Science Fair. He goes on to become an acclaimed NASA rocket scientist. In one of the key scenes in the movie, he states very clearly that mining isn't for him. His father, an intimidating and highly respected supervisor at the mine, roars, "Boy, you don't know what the mine gives you!" It's the father-son disconnect at its most acute. Despite the fact that the mine ultimately kills the father (black lung disease) and the school in the mining town is nothing other than an incubator for future miners and housewives, the father's reaction is telling. Yes, working at the mine paid the father a living wage. What he doesn't say, but becomes clear, is that his very identity is tied to how good he is at his job. People depend on him for their safety and their livelihood. He is the proverbial *big man* in this little town. He loves his job with a stubborn pride that is disconnected from the actual misery of working in and around a mine. What he might have said is, "Boy, you don't know what the mine gives *me*!"

First of all, I hope that you don't work in a coal mine. Second of all, if you do, stop. Please find the nearest exit and if at all possible, find a job that doesn't have you breathing coal dust. We've all heard stories about the worker who toils away for years fantasizing about retirement, and then when that much-anticipated day finally arrives, he spends a few days sipping lemonade on the front porch and then passes away. You can visualize his soul flying away in protest over being severed from his work identity. The reality is less dire, but I've found that clients do need to think hard about whether retirement is really the right choice for them. It's easy enough to brush this aside. After all, shouldn't everyone love the idea of unshackling themselves from the grind of the workplace? Maybe not.

First, I want you to circle the items on this list that you appreciate about work. Sideline our ultimate goal of *joy* for the moment. That's the mountaintop, and we're just starting to climb. For now, just circle the positives:

(a) Nice paycheck

(b) Expense account

(c) Work friendships

(d) Creative or intellectual stimulation

(e) Making a difference

(f) The pride that comes with being good at what I do

If you only circled (a) and (b), congratulations on your upcoming retirement! Get your financial ducks in a row (hopefully with the help of this book), give your colleagues a hug, and get the heck out of Dodge.

If you circled (c), (d), (e), or (f), we still have work to do.

While a nice paycheck and an expense account merit little explanation, let's examine the other positives in more detail.

<u>Work Friendships.</u> Ah yes, the sometimes wonderful, sometimes awkward work friendship. A workplace friend can range from that

younger party animal you felt compelled to "hang" with at the Las Vegas sales convention because she's your superior and she wants to assess whether you're uptight (i.e., not much of a friendship) to the fellow professor with whom you worked for thirty years on your Nobel-prize winning theorem, and whose children are your godchildren, and whose husband is also your husband's best friend (i.e., you are inseparable). If it's the latter, fear not, unless a geographic move takes you far away and you are allergic to travel, your friendship will certainly survive retirement. If it's the former, the relationship won't last, and that's a good thing. After all, it might be best if you never again find yourself wobbling around Las Vegas at 3:00 a.m. with Generation Never-Sleep.

Friends who fall somewhere between the two extremes I've painted are the friends you may wind up missing. These are folks who you genuinely enjoyed and confided in, but who will slip away once you leave your job behind. It's that super-funny colleague who had you in stitches over lunch twice a week, but who you won't expect to just "drop by" once you've left your job, or that insanely smart research assistant who continually kept you on your toes, and who never failed to ask about your family (and actually listened when you responded).

Losing casual work friendships and the associated social stimulation can be isolating for many. If you're retiring early, you need to be particularly careful about this. You may be ready for retirement, while your friends outside of work may not have the same capacity to spend time together. Imagine you have three close friends outside of work, and when you announce that you are officially retired and ready to play, they glance nervously at each other with an expression that says, "Will you tell her, or should I?" Maybe they aren't ready to retire, or maybe they simply have a very different idea regarding the amount of time you will spend together.

If the vast majority of your friendships are work friendships, and you don't want to risk struggling with loneliness in retirement, I suggest that you systematically start the process of developing new friendships outside of work. Yes, I did use the word systematically, and it's not because I am a robot. Finding new friends can feel like an awkward form of dating, but it's critically important, even for my fellow introverts. Having a handful of friends with common interests at the ready when you hang up work once and for all is a winning strategy, and while it comes naturally to some, it is a labor-intensive process for others.

If your best friends are from high school or college, you likely benefited from the fact that you were thrown together in one of the world's greatest social experiments. Said differently, you were forced into close contact with a very large group of individuals your own age. Even introverts in high school and college find their people. Along the same lines, I've never met anyone who served in the military who couldn't cite at least a handful of friendships that were forged under duress (whether it's the unique bond forged between fellow soldiers in combat, or whether it's simply the bond that comes from suffering through basic training or being deployed around the globe together).

The point is this: No one is going to push you out the door in your retirement years and force you to interact with like-minded people. Developing friendships is an important task, and often a hard one. Here are a few ideas for finding new friends:

Go Online. Yes, I said it. For the younger readers of this book, this comes as no surprise. Finding a loved one online is certainly quite common, and there are a number of websites that facilitate meeting new (non-romantic) friends. Here are a few: Meetup.com, which allows users to sort through groups of people across thousands of cities who share similar interests and/or similar ages;

Nextdoor.com, which allows users to connect with neighbors more easily; and Friender.com, which suggests friend matches for you based on geography and interests.

Volunteer. If you are passionate about a particular cause, by volunteering your time at local events, you may find yourself quickly immersed in a new group of like-minded friends. Wielding a hammer while building homes for the underprivileged is a fine way to connect with fellow charitable souls. Just promise me you won't accept the role of roofer if you're over the age of seventy. Beach clean-up trips, meal preparation services, nursing home visits, museum docent duties—the list of possibilities goes on and on.

Hobby Groups. I'll comment on hobbies in more detail later, but why not join a group of fellow surfers, bocce ballers, knitters, archers, golfers, painters, or Dungeon and Dragons players? If you're willing to hop online, you'll have no trouble tracking down folks who share your passion for a particular hobby—unless, of course, your hobby involves restoring 17th century harpsichords, in which case you may have to search a bit further afield for fellow aficionados.

Creative or Intellectual Stimulation. If you're a hired hand at the poultry processing plant, I will go out on a limb and predict that there is little chance that you find your work intellectually stimulating. If you're an astrophysicist at the top of her game, who enjoys academic sparring with all of the up-and-coming eggheads (I use this term fondly), you may wring more intellectual stimulation out of any given week than most of us do in our entire working careers.

Here I will use a personal example that is near and dear to my heart. My father, who is eighty years old, is revered by many in his organization for his wisdom, experience, and ability to translate insanely complicated physics problems into language mere mortals (like me) can almost understand. He is casually referred to by younger employees as Obi-Wan, and he engages in regular discussions about his broad array of world-changing projects with none other than Bill Gates, Nathan Myhrvold, and other tech luminaries whose intellect is legendary.

My father's professional survival is contingent on his ability to keep up with some of the sharpest minds around. If you could gauge the intellectual stimulation he receives at work on a scale of one to ten, the needle on his gauge would tremble violently right at ten. While I suspect that my father could retire, I don't know that he should retire. Hard work is what he has always known, and he loves his work dearly. If he passed away at ninety with whiteboard marker in hand, explaining the challenges of developing a fission reactor powered by existing nuclear waste to a young engineer, I suspect he would die a happy man.

How do you feel about the intellectual challenges you face at work? Do they keep you sharp, or are you able to breeze through your daily tasks with ease? Try to gauge how much you appreciate the intellectual workout you receive at work and whether or not you can achieve something equally stimulating in retirement. Poetry writing, anyone? Rebuilding that 1967 Mustang in the garage? Or how about mastering the art of astral navigation? That will keep you busy for quite some time. We'll discuss hobbies in more detail later.

Making a Difference. We can all define "making a difference" differently, but do you find your work particularly meaningful? What makes it more than just a paycheck? While someone who sells timeshares using high-pressure sales tactics might not be able to say with a straight face that he or she is improving the human condition, the senior researcher working diligently on a cure for cancer probably can.

Those who find their work deeply meaningful may have a harder time transitioning to retirement. Consider the classic case of the retiring admiral. He spent the last four years of his career commanding one hundred thousand sailors and over two thousand ships in the Pacific. Many decisions he made had a direct impact on the lives of his subordinates, his influence in the appropriations process resulted in the allocation of billions of dollars, and his counsel helped craft U.S. foreign policy. Now that he's considering retirement, he can't even get his adult children to give him the time of day. They love him, but they're just too busy with their own lives. While remaining employed as an admiral may not be a possibility, he may find that he can continue to make a difference by serving on the board of a non-profit, or perhaps by joining one of the many think tanks in Washington D.C.

If retirement is optional at this point, carefully weigh the freedom of being able to do what you like (and presumably run your own schedule) against the knowledge that your work makes a difference in the world. Are you really done, or will you miss the sense of accomplishment you derive from your work too much if you leave it behind?

Pride. You are good at what you do. Your colleagues know it, you know it, and it naturally results in a sense of pride in your work. Maybe no engineer understands the complex inner workings of the Los Angeles County Landfill better than you, or maybe no other professor can more swiftly decipher whether an aspiring novelist displays the talent of a young James Joyce than you. Regardless of your skillset, if you're good at what you do, letting go of the affirmation you receive from work can be hard.

As you review the list of positives that come from your work, think hard about how much they mean to you and what it will require to find a decent substitute in retirement. Try ranking the positives according to importance (high, medium, low) and the amount of work required to find a substitute (hard, moderate, easy). For those of you who like lists and tables, creating a table may prove useful. You can find a blank table in the appendix. The following table is for an accomplished surgeon considering retirement.

	Working Years (Value)	Retirement (Ease of Replacement)
Work Friendships	*Medium*: As a surgeon, I value my friendships with fellow physicians. While I would only rank two fellow physicians as close friends, I could name a dozen colleagues I will miss.	*Hard*: I need to work on my friendships outside of work. I currently have few hobbies, and I risk feeling isolated. I am also a bit of an introvert. This is going to take work, and I will likely focus on making friendships based on new interests/activities. This is a top priority, and while I don't need a huge network of friends, developing a few close friendships will be critical.

	Working Years (Value)	Retirement (Ease of Replacement)
Creative or Intellectual Stimulation	*Medium*: My work is challenging, and I do need to stay on top of the latest research and techniques. That being said, my focus is narrow, and after operating for 25 years, I've largely got it sorted out.	*Moderate*: I love to read stimulating non-fiction (science is a favorite), and back when I had time, I liked building things. Building a wooden boat from plans sounds labor-intensive and rewarding. I have a shop full of tools I never use.
Making a Difference	*High*: The cliché holds true. Lives hang in the balance. My work has a profound impact on patients and their families.	*Easy*: While I won't be saving lives on a daily basis, I think I just need to recalibrate a bit. I am deeply interested in education, and I want to mentor disadvantaged youth in my area. I'm confident I'll figure this out after a bit of soul searching and exploring opportunities in my area.

	Working Years (Value)	Retirement (Ease of Replacement)
Pride/Self-Esteem	*Low*: I am an expert in my field, and of course I would be lying if I didn't admit that the positive feedback is nice. I hope I am not deceiving myself here, but I feel like I'm past this. Early in my career this was immensely important to me. Now I think I'm comfortable putting this behind me.	*Hard*: What can I say about this? I don't think the positive feedback from a long career as a surgeon can be replicated. I'll work hard to become known as a great volunteer/ philanthropist.

In summary, my physician client knows he is excellent at what he does, but he doesn't cherish the self-esteem that comes from his work as others might. He's also confident that he will find great personal meaning through volunteer work, and while he's far behind in terms of developing interests outside of work, he is confident that his thirst for knowledge and his interest in at least one very challenging project will keep his mind fully engaged. The biggest hurdle faced by this client is developing friendships. He acknowledges that it is going to be hard, and he may need to work at developing friendships in a disciplined/systematic manner.

Know thyself. Without dropping further into annoying clichés, I simply want to make a critical point here. The drill we've immersed ourselves in is really about self-awareness. I want you to fully understand what work offers you and what you may be leaving behind if you elect to retire early. If you make the transition into retirement with your eyes wide open, the possibility of creating a joyful epilogue to your working life increases exponentially.

All or Nothing? Well, hold on a second. Who ever said retirement has to be an all-or-nothing proposition? For some, a gradual ratcheting down of the demands of work over time is not only achievable, but highly desirable. Before we get excited about the possibility of a part-time gig, we need to examine whether it is a realistic possibility. The sad truth is that while some careers are highly scalable, others simply aren't. Here are a few examples, from highly scalable employment to all-or-nothing propositions.

Highly Scalable. Individuals in jobs that are highly scalable are in a great position to consider the possibility of working well into their retirement years, albeit at a greatly reduced pace.

Example 1: The Therapist. My wife, Janelle, is a Marriage and Family Therapist with a successful solo practice. She sets her own hours, only works with whom she wishes to work, and generally runs her practice as she chooses. She doesn't deal with insurance (which makes her practice a source of envy for some therapists), and scheduling is fairly straightforward, which means that the administrative burden of running her practice is minimal. While there are indeed minimum continuing education requirements for her work, she would attend these classes out of interest regardless. She commands a healthy hourly rate, and she only needs to work two hours per week to cover her overhead (which is limited to office rent, malpractice insurance, and continuing education). In short, if you could design a professional practice perfectly suited to part-time work, it would be hers. She loves her job, and seeing three clients a day three days a week is a pace she may be able to sustain into her eighties (presuming good health).

Example 2: The Emergency Room Physician. I have worked with many clients who are either physicians or nurses who receive competitive pay for part-time work. While many medical groups/hospitals may not offer this possibility, a particular client, who is a Kaiser emergency room physician, immediately comes to mind. In his mid-fifties, recognizing that his work (though quite rewarding) was exhausting, he explored the possibility of working half-time. Not a problem, came the response from Kaiser, and so my client continued to enjoy the intellectual stimulation, camaraderie, sense of purpose, and pay that comes with being an emergency room physician, all while inserting plenty of breathing room and recuperation into his schedule. This came with a further benefit. The extra time off allowed him to focus on developing his interests and friendships outside of work—a major head-start when it comes to preparing for full retirement.

<u>Somewhat Scalable.</u> Individuals with partially scalable jobs may indeed be able to craft a plan for fulfilling part-time work, but a bit more effort/complexity is involved.

Example 1: *The Consultant.* Consulting can be challenging work, and for many, the demands of work involve travel, long hours, and maintaining the agility to quickly respond to client demands. While some consultants make it very clear that their work is either 110 percent or nothing, many others indicate that they can pick or choose their projects. Presumably, this is a byproduct of either (a) the consultant's professional reputation—i.e., clients will flex to meet the needs of a highly-sought-after consultant, or (b) the nature of the industry and the particular flavor of consulting—i.e., some forms of consulting are geared toward crisis management, while others allow a bit more advance planning.

Regardless, I call consulting "partially scalable" because while part-time work is indeed possible for many consultants, I've learned that dialing back the work meter can result in very uneven workflow. Said differently, instead of simply working fewer hours a day (the therapist) or fewer hours in a week (the emergency room physician), consultants may take on fewer projects, but sometimes the demands of the projects themselves remain constant. This means that in Month A the consultant may work fifty hours per week on a pressing project, while in Month B the consultant may not work at all. To be clear, some people love this pace of work—either they are grinding it out in a conference room, or they are sitting on a beach in Hawaii—while others find that it simply becomes too exhausting as they grow older.

Example 2: The Lawyer. I have to be very careful with this one. At most large international law firms (I used to work at one), the notion of part-time work is a thinly disguised fiction. The demands placed on partners by clients who are willing to pay top dollar for legal work are simply too high for part-time employment. If you're an attorney commanding $1,000 per hour for your work with various corporate clients, those clients naturally expect something in return, and that something is often your complete availability and responsiveness (i.e., your soul). There are exceptions to this rule, of course. Nevertheless, for an example of a partially scalable legal practice, I'll focus on an estate-planning practitioner. While clients do actually die, and this may dictate that an attorney ramp up her work at an unpredictable time, estate planners generally have fairly scalable, low-key practices. Slowly ratcheting back work by passing cases to another attorney is indeed possible. The reason this practice is only partially scalable is that the overhead for many legal practices is high. A secretary, a paralegal, substantial rent, a malpractice policy, various subscriptions to drafting software and/or research tools… The list goes on and on. At some point, an attorney will only be working to cover overhead.

<u>Non-Scalable.</u> Unfortunately, many jobs in corporate America fall into this category. A non-scalable job is an all-or-nothing proposition. In other words, an employee must either devote a

huge amount of energy and effort to her position or fully retire from the job.

Example 1: The Corporate Sales Manager. I've worked with many clients who are successful managers of sales representatives at large technology companies. The paychecks these clients receive can be quite enticing, but the pace of work is universally frenetic. When I ask a client who is a vice president of sales at a large technology company how work is treating him, I might expect to hear, "Great! I only had to work three Saturdays this month." Sales is often a numbers game, and it can be both thrilling and exceptionally demanding. Is it possible to work part-time as a vice president of sales for a large company? "No" is the resounding feedback I've received. "Never gonna happen."

Example 2: The Professional Athlete. While clearly this profession is the domain of a select few highly talented individuals, my hope is that this example will illustrate an important point. Some professions require more than competence—instead, they require near-monk-like devotion and a level of excellence that is only sustainable with full-time effort. Can a professional basketball player attend only half of the team practices and selectively choose which games to attend? Not to my knowledge. Likewise, can a Formula 1 driver afford to let her skillset slip a bit? Nope. She'll die in a raging inferno after losing control on Turn 2. In both examples, while the profession itself is entirely non-scalable, professional athletes may have an opportunity to parlay their reputation and skillset into a fulfilling second career, which is the topic of the next section.

Take a moment to think about your profession and whether it is highly scalable, partially scalable, or non-scalable. If you have a highly scalable job and you find yourself getting teary-eyed over the thought of leaving behind the intellectual stimulation, sense of purpose, or friendships that come with your work, I strongly suggest that you consider a few years of part-time employment. Not only will the additional income be nice, but you'll also have more time during which to work on building new friendships, developing hobbies, etc. For many, this is the best possible transition into full retirement.

If you have a partially scalable job, part-time work *might* be appealing. To fully unravel whether part-time work is worth considering or not, think through the reasons you are considering retiring in the first place. Are you simply exhausted from the frantic pace of work? If so, is it realistic to believe that you can create breathing room by taking on additional projects (in the case of the consultant) or working fewer hours (in the case of the estate-planning attorney)? If this is the case, you might consider giving part-time work a shot. If you've simply lost interest in your job, and that is what is driving your decision to retire, part-time work doesn't make much sense. Why do less of the unenjoyable thing when you can eliminate the unenjoyable thing entirely? If there is no joy in your work, and you can afford to fully retire, the answer may be an easy one. You're done.

A Second Career. Let's say you've ruled out the possibility of ratcheting back your work schedule, either because your job isn't scalable or because you're simply done and ready to move on. Rather than sailing into the sunset on your brand-new yacht and sipping Mai Tais in the Virgin Islands, maybe you should consider the possibility that another type of work will be more to your liking. Perhaps you've heard stories like this:

Example 1: The Pilot. Even after logging millions of miles as an airline pilot, Sheila hasn't lost her love of planes. She's ready to retire from the slog of crossing the Pacific in a 747, but she feels compelled to combine her skill as a pilot with something that brings her joy, a little bit of income (emphasis on *little*), and perhaps some intellectual stimulation and camaraderie. Sheila retires to a scenic town with an airstrip deep inside California's wine country, buys herself a vintage bi-plane, and offers rides to eager passengers. Maintaining her plane keeps her mind busy, hanging out with the other pilots who frequent the airport means she has a ready-made group of friends, and flying upside down over gorgeous green hills bursting with clusters of ripe grapes brings her immense joy. What about her sense of purpose? To be clear, this wonderful career transition need not be tied to some altruistic motive. But fear not, Sheila's got that whole "giving back" thing covered too. She offers free rides to high schoolers from poorer neighborhoods who think that they want to become pilots. The few that can keep their lunch down after getting the inverted 'Sheila treatment' are doubly committed to getting their pilot's license.

Example 2: The CEO. After years of running a large public company, Jacob retires early, gets his teaching credential, and then teaches AP physics to a crowd of rowdy high schoolers. He finds teaching high schoolers rewarding in ways that differ from the satisfaction he used to get from running a company. He is shaping young souls, preparing them for the substantial challenges they will face when they inherit our planet. Sounds wonderful, doesn't it? Jacob lasts two years. Teaching is hard. He continues to support his local high school by volunteering his time and donating generously, but he chooses to spend more of his time in retirement golfing and playing his Steinway. And you know what? There is absolutely nothing wrong with that.

The point of my story about Jacob is that once you've established that you can retire early, you have incredible freedom. The pressure is off. If you like your new job, great. If you find a new job exhausting and subsequently decide that full-blown retirement is the answer, at least you'll be more confident in your decision to hang it up for good.

When contemplating a career change, learn everything you can about the new direction you're headed. Is additional education required, or perhaps a credential? Do you have the energy required to make this new career worthwhile? It's easy to romanticize certain professions (a la Jacob and teaching high-school physics), but don't forget to ask those who are currently employed in the field about the nitty-gritty details. What do they dislike about their job? What advice would they offer to someone who is considering a late transition into the field?

We've spent a great deal of time analyzing whether fully retiring will restrict elements in your life that have brought you joy. If you decide to either (a) fully retire, or (b) work part-time, you'll have a lot of free time to fill. This is a bigger obstacle than most soon-to-be retired individuals recognize. Let's start with an easy concept: hobbies and passions.

<u>Hobbies and Passions.</u> The very word hobby seems a bit antiquated in certain circles. When I ask my Silicon Valley workaholics about their hobbies, I often get a blank look in response. If not a vacant stare, I might get the following, "Well… I went to Burning Man this year." Attending Burning Man in an air-conditioned RV and spending several days contemplating the universe while tripping on mushrooms does not a hobby make. That's called *fun*, and only Timothy Leary could have called it his hobby, though *vocation* might have been a better word in his case.

When I use the word "hobby," I mean something you can do regularly that brings you great pleasure and doesn't involve ingesting illegal substances. Wine tasting can certainly qualify, but only if you really study the finer points of winemaking (i.e., you don't just stumble on and off the party bus as you make the obligatory stops on Napa Valley Road). Woodworking, piano, gardening, building stuff, sailing, cooking, needlepoint, camping, photography, chess, book club, bocce ball, biking, archery, bird watching… The list of possibilities goes on and on. My semi-retired mother-in-law became a champion pickleball player and made many new friends in the process.

Maybe you can think of a handful of activities that you've enjoyed over the years, but none of them yet qualify as hobbies, and certainly not as passions. As you explore the possibility of sinking more time into any particular activity, here are a few things I'd like you to consider.

The Cost Factor. I'm a financial planner, so I feel compelled to mention cost. Before you get too deeply involved, I suggest that you put the ixnay on your plan to collect Fabergé eggs. Think about the impact of your burgeoning hobby on your bottom line. Enough said. Anyway, Fabergé eggs are *so* 19th century.

The Joy Factor. Ah yes, the joy factor. Have you toyed with various hobbies that are kinda sorta fun, but also a wee bit boring? Ixnay! (At least for now.) We are seeking joy, my friend, not simply a task to occupy your time. This should be a fun thought-project. Close your eyes, take a few deep breaths, and bring yourself back to a time you felt pure, unadulterated joy. Where were you? Who were you with? What were you doing?

There are certainly joyful memories that may come up that don't translate into a hobby (cough, cough), but if you flip through that catalogue of amazing life experiences, a few may materialize that involve a distinct activity that can be replicated. Maybe it was harvesting that first bumper crop of tomatoes from your garden. Maybe it was hiking on the beach with your best friend. Maybe it was laughing until you cried with a posse of fellow bibliophiles at your weekly book club gathering. Maybe it was spotting an ivory-billed woodpecker after roaming the Arkansas forests for weeks searching for this most elusive of birds. Go ahead—jot down a few ideas and focus on how they made you feel then, and then spend a moment imagining doing them now.

The Sustainability Factor—aka the Capacity Dilemma. Unfortunately, the relentless march of time is something you should consider when deciding where to focus your efforts. If you are already a big-wave surfer, and you just know that you have another ten years of shredding left in you, I say *go for it.* But if twenty years ago you surfed a gentle two-foot wave in Oahu, now you live in Half Moon Bay, California, and you're thinking about giving surfing another try in your retirement years, please leave the thirty-foot swells to the professionals. While falling down the face of a monster wave might be a glorious curtain call, I want you to embrace your retirement years, not end them prematurely.

Some hobbies and passions translate quite nicely into retirement. Others don't. There is a reason golf courses are overrun with retirees (though the sport can be hard on the back). There is also a reason ice climbers over age seventy are as rare as red-crowned cranes. Think about the sustainability of your interests. Is it likely you can continue to pursue a particular hobby into your sixties, seventies, eighties?

The Social Factor. Remember, retirement can be isolating, and loneliness is a killer. I'm quite serious about this. Loneliness has a bigger impact on longevity than most of us would suspect. Further, it's a problem that is so prevalent that the United Kingdom created a Ministry of Loneliness to deal with the problem (I kid you not). Even introverts need periodic social stimulation, and hobbies are not only a nice way to get you out of the house, but they are also a great way to make lasting friendships. Perhaps your hobbies are solitary activities that don't appear to offer a great deal of opportunity to socialize. Fear not—it's likely those traditionally solitary hobbies can be reconstrued as group events. Enjoy reading? Join a book club. Enjoy gardening? Join a gardening club.

As a shy teenager, I was always drawn to activities that I could perform on my own. I ran thousands of miles solo on mountain trails. I surfed. I played the piano. I developed a passion for writing. In my golden years, will you find me sprinting down mountainsides without a partner? Nope. I can already visualize the mountain lion gnawing on my shin as I lay at the bottom of a ravine in a crumpled heap. But would I enjoy hiking in the mountains with my fellow retirees? Sure would. Similarly, writing has always been a solitary endeavor for me. It's also something I hope to continue to do well into retirement. Though it will force me out of my comfort zone, I'm certain I'll find my way into a writer's workshop.

But enough about me. This is about you. I want you to embrace hobbies that are affordable, joyful, sustainable, and offer you a social outlet. And you get bonus points if a hobby happens to be intellectually stimulating as well. Sounds nice, you think, but maybe you really don't have any hobbies. Maybe your life has always been about your job and your family, and a hobby just felt like an indulgence.

Well, okay then. Are you willing to learn? Sorry, that shouldn't be a question, but a statement. You <u>are</u> willing to learn. How do I know? You're reading this book, and if you've made it this far, you have more discipline than the average Joe.

Now, on to a topic that may be either (a) near and dear to your heart, or (b) irrelevant. If you select (b), please skip this chapter. Next up is how your retirement will impact your relationship with family.

Family

First, I'd like to observe with deep sincerity that if your family is a huge source of joy in your life, you've already won. Stop for a moment and think about this. All of the money and free time in the world will never come close to the feeling you get by both loving your family and being loved by your family. Are you sensing my soft side? I'm getting misty-eyed as I write this. Lifelong bachelors and bachelorettes, the next section may not be critical in the short-term, but who knows what life will bring!

The Complex Partnership Dynamic. Retiring can have a profound impact on the health of a committed romantic relationship (which I'll generically refer to as a marriage). To understand why, let's explore the odyssey of John, a recently retired sales executive, and Stacy, his stay-at-home spouse.

John is a hustler. In elementary school he went door-to-door and asked anyone who answered if he could mow their lawn for a quarter. In high school he woke up at 5:00 a.m. to deliver newspapers and worked in construction all summer. He started honing his sales skills right out of high school (cutlery, again door-to-door), but quickly realized life had bigger plans for him. John was savvy, and he could smell an opportunity a mile away. *Software sales.* The commissions were huge and the competition was stiff, but he knew he would somehow break into the profession. He tirelessly sought employment in the field while working toward a bachelor's degree at night.

Fast-forward many years. John never lost his drive. His travel schedule was relentless, but he could close a deal like no one else, and he was paid very handsomely for it. In the meantime, Stacy, his wife of thirty years, raised two wonderful children, served on the PTA and the homeowner's association board, cared for John's elderly parents as well as her own, and supported John in a myriad of ways.

John often fantasized about retirement. The thought of leaving behind the pressure of aggressive sales targets and the exhaustion of red-eye flights was almost too foreign to fully process. But then one day it was all over. Instead of excitement, during his first week of retirement John experienced something akin to a panic attack. He was crawling in his own skin, intermittently pacing around the house like a madman and then flipping through television channels at a relentless pace.

In the meantime, after thirty years of running the household her own way, Stacy desperately tried to adjust to having this manic creature in her home. She cleaned up after John constantly (she hates a messy home), prepared not just one family meal a day (the old routine) but three, and responded to his repeated requests to help him find one thing or another. He could *never* find anything. It was maddening.

In the past, Stacy treasured the first hour after John and the kids left the house each morning. It was her time to herself. She could actually get stuff done, and the quiet was wonderful. That was gone now. She felt like she was waiting on John hand and foot, and the man was clearly miserable. In fact, they were both miserable.

Stacy loved John deeply. If you asked her to describe her husband, she'd smile and say, "He's a *good* man." But she couldn't shake the feeling that she had just adopted a man-child, and she wasn't eager to experience Motherhood Part II. Combined with John's sudden insistence on constant physical attention, she was at her wit's ends. The thought of separating even crossed her mind.

Stacy and John were in big trouble. They had been so focused on raising their children and saving for retirement that they neglected to consider what life would be like once John stopped working. John didn't have many friends outside of work, and he had no hobbies other than golf (which was a professional requirement, he liked to say). Conversely, Stacy had a vibrant group of girlfriends. They walked together, lunched together, commiserated together, laughed together, and cried together. She had been quite content with her life prior to John's retirement.

Time to call in the rescue squad. On to the present day. Stacy drags a very reluctant John to a couple's counselor. At first John is crushed when he realizes that he is making his wife miserable. But through some hard work and a great deal of introspection, John concludes that he needs to make some changes. The counselor helps him create a plan to get out of the house, develop new interests, and make new friends. She also helps John recalibrate his expectations of Stacy. Stacy doesn't want to be his mother. John's increased appetite for physical attention is tragically colliding head-on with the rapid diminishment of Stacy' attraction to him, and both Stacy and John agree that this merits immediate attention.

Is all hope lost for our couple? Will they become another data point in the rapidly rising divorce rate among retirees? No way. They've been through too much together. Remember, Stacy and John love each other deeply, and John is a workhorse. John devotes his relentless energy to the task of repairing their relationship, and guess what? It works.

John rekindles an interest in the Civil War that dates back to high school. He starts reading obsessively, and before too long, he finds himself in a Union uniform learning how to prep a muzzle loader for combat. It's a whole crazy world, this reenactment thing. Before long John has a new bestie, Stan, who loves both golf and anything related to the Civil War. Stan also loves sailing, and after slapping a Dramamine patch on John, they take to the water. A new passion is born.

Watching John blossom in retirement is rekindling Stacy's old attraction to the man. While she resolutely refuses to dress in a Union nurse's costume (that civil war stuff can be *his* thing), she is an enthusiastic supporter of his new sailing hobby. And Stacy wasn't just an idle observer during those therapy sessions. For her part, she has learned to draw clear boundaries—yes, she'll prepare meals, but not three a day—and no, she is not going to drop what she is doing and spend the next thirty minutes looking for John's missing sock. Date nights are mandatory—at least one per week—and she is also careful to schedule girls-only outings on a regular basis.

Whew... A close call, wasn't it? I don't want this to be you. To avoid John and Stacy' brush with disaster, I suggest that you sit down with your spouse and discuss the following potential issues in detail. You don't need to create a twenty-page retirement plan, but you should give each applicable topic a fair amount of thought.

Retirement Goals. You plan to visit a dozen countries in the first two years of retirement. Your spouse wants to hang out with the grandkids at the lake house. You want to die penniless at age 102, confident that you have squeezed every last bit of joy out of those hard-earned dollars. Your spouse wants to leave a million dollars to each child. You desperately want to learn to ballroom dance, and your spouse would sooner endure a root canal.

You get the idea. It is critically important you and your spouse discuss your goals in retirement. I am dismayed by how many couples don't actually do this. Staring at each other on that first day of retirement with a shrug and the mumbled question, "What now?" is not a good plan. Instead, talk about your retirement goals well in advance, and be prepared to flex a bit. You love your spouse. Let's make sure you both get your needs met. Here are a few questions I suggest that you discuss:

- Where will you live? You might find that one of you anticipates that you will stay in your current home, while the other secretly harbors a desire to move closer to your children.

- What about travel? Do you both fantasize about that month-long bicycle tour of southern France, or is that only an entry on *your* bucket list? If your children live elsewhere, how often will you visit? And where will you stay—in their house, or in a hotel?

- How much time will you spend apart, and how will you structure this? Do you even need time apart? (Most couples do, of course, but there are exceptions, like those lovely couples that could pass for identical twins separated at birth. You know, the ones who finish each other's sentences and silently share the remote control in an eerie telepathic dance).

- How will you share responsibility for household chores? If you both worked full-time and are miraculously retiring at the same time, it may be that nothing needs to change. However, if one of you is a homemaker and the other is employed full-time, brace yourself for an epic household-chore shakedown. I suggest you get it out of the way now.

- After many happy years of an active retirement, how do the two of you plan to handle potential disability or the need for assistance? Said differently, does one of you relish the thought of joining the Ukulele Club at that assisted living facility down the road, while the other would prefer to don a wingsuit and jump off El Capitan without a parachute?

> Joking aside, this is a very important issue for retiring couples. If you're committed to staying together (which I hope is the case), you better make sure you're on the same page about living arrangements in your final years.

Breathing Room. My hope is that you and your spouse love each other dearly, and that even after thirty years together, your first thought each morning and your last thought each night centers around an overwhelming sense of gratitude at having found the perfect partner. While spending huge amounts of time together in retirement may feel like a positive, I do want you to consider the possibility that you will periodically need a bit of breathing room.

I've found that some couples are very good at this, and it comes naturally. For example, when Brian and Brenda get tired of each other, Brenda either spends time in the garden or schedules bonding time with her sister (and best friend), and Billy either goes on an all-day walkabout in the hills or catches a movie in town. If a longer break from each other is needed, they don't hesitate to schedule short separate vacations.

Whatever your mechanism for creating a bit of breathing room in retirement, make sure you've thought this through prior to leaving the workforce. Seeing your spouse on weekends and for a few hours on weekday evenings is very different than the 24-7 facetime that can follow retirement. You've heard the expression, "Distance makes the heart grow fonder." While not always true, periodic time apart may help keep the flame of passion burning in that love-struck heart of yours.

Timing of Retirement—Simultaneous or Staggered. Clearly you and your spouse should think carefully about the timing of your retirement. After all, we've spent many pages reviewing the financial and emotional implications of leaving the workforce. What we haven't discussed, however, is how to best handle the *order of retirement* issue if both you and your spouse are employed. Put simply, which one of you gets to retire first? While the financial element of this drill is important and may heavily impact your balance sheet and cash-flow projections, I want to touch on the less frequently discussed emotional implications of this decision.

Perhaps you and your spouse are both employed, and while you can both tolerate your jobs, the thought of leaving the workforce is equally appealing to each of you. To level the playing field even further, let's imagine that you both have the ability to provide employer-sponsored health insurance for the other for as long as you work. Should you try to pull-off a near-simultaneous retirement, or is a staggered approach to retirement more desirable? There's no easy answer here, of course, so let's discuss the pros and cons of each, along with the strategies for making either approach mutually beneficial.

Staggered Retirement. One sizable benefit of staggering your respective retirement ages is obvious. The extra income and continued medical coverage that comes with one of you continuing to work can be helpful. A less obvious benefit: one of you will get to prepare extensively for the 24-7 facetime conundrum we discussed earlier. In other words, the one of you who retires first will be able to devote a significant amount of time to strengthening friendships, exploring various hobbies, and otherwise getting better at managing that potentially alien phenomenon known as "free time" without an ever-present spouse complicating things.

Unfortunately, staggering your retirement ages can give rise to several problems as well. Remember, I am assuming that you both *want* to retire, and the sooner the better. First of all, how in the world do you decide who gets to go first? And second, presuming you can make that decision, how do you avoid having the result of this decision grow into a source of resentment?

The answer to the first question: communicate, and then communicate some more. By the time you play out the decision of who gets to retire first, I want this to be such a tired topic that you can't possibly tolerate another word on the subject. I could devote an entire book to the art of active listening, the win-win mindset, fighting fairly, and other critical elements of what I'll call "relationship management." Presumably that's not why you picked up this book, so I'll keep it punchy.

When your spouse tries to articulate why he wants to retire first, *really* listen. I mean listen *actively*. In other words, don't just repeat back word-for-word what your spouse said (an unfair trick), but instead listen carefully, ask for clarification when needed, and try to empathize. If you get stuck—you are both human, after all—I strongly recommend that you consider working with a couples counselor to help you through this discussion.

Now, on to the topic of avoiding resentment once the decision about who gets to retire first has been made. This doesn't have to be a winner-take-all proposition. Remember, this is your beloved spouse we're talking about, and therefore the notion of a win-win solution should be particularly appealing. If you've both worked for decades, it may be that neither of you has any sense of what it's like to have a stay-at-home spouse. What if the one who agrees to keep grinding it out for a few more years gets to experience a *few* of the benefits of having a stay-at-home spouse? Here's an example of what I mean:

Melinda and Bill are both successful managers at large companies, and they've both dreamed ceaselessly about retiring for several years. After an extensive discussion with their therapist (good job, Bill and Melinda), they determine that Melinda will retire first. Melinda is absolutely ecstatic that Bill is willing to keep working for two more years. The continued medical coverage will be nice, and several big expenses that are keeping Melinda up at night are approaching rapidly (including in-home nursing care for her mother and a wedding for their daughter). Melinda fully recognizes the sacrifice that Bill is making, and she is deeply committed to showing him how much it means to her.

In addition to taking time to strengthen her friendships and develop new hobbies, Melinda devotes a few hours a day to improving the quality of Bill's life. Back when they both worked fifty-hour weeks, take-out meals were the rule, not the exception. One of Melinda's new hobbies is cooking, and she begins taking great pride in creating spectacular meals for the two of them. In addition, while Bill used to take the lead on planning vacations, Melinda assumes this job with gusto and carefully plans a series of romantic weekend getaways.

Like Bill and Melinda, if you and your spouse decide that one of you gets to retire first, I hope that this improves both of your lives. But maybe you're on the fence about this whole notion of staggering your retirement dates. Well, what about the advantages and disadvantages of retiring simultaneously?

Assuming that you and your spouse both really *want* to retire (and soon), retiring simultaneously has an obvious emotional advantage. It is presumably fair. Although I'm certain there are exceptions, retiring at the same time doesn't seem likely to generate resentment. Further, retiring simultaneously has one additional potentially significant advantage. For adventurous couples, retiring simultaneously allows you to hit the road (or the sea, or the sky) sooner rather than later. If you've both dreamed of sailing the Mediterranean for several years immediately following retirement, staggering your retirement dates may not make any sense. If you can afford to retire simultaneously, carpe diem.

Simultaneous retirement does have a potentially significant emotional drawback, and because I've already walked you through this issue with an example, I'll simply re-state the problem. Going from 60mph (your work schedule) to zero (retirement) can be very problematic for less adventurous couples. Maybe neither of you was able to heed my advice and begin easing the transition into retirement by focusing on (and developing) non-work-related sources of joy in your life. I hope this isn't you, but what if you find yourself sitting in your La-Z-Boy in your air-conditioned house in Sun City, staring at your spouse blankly while the television drones on in the background? Unfortunately, you run the very real risk of making each other miserable. If one of you retires early, being *truly* alone (as opposed to simply *feeling* alone while sitting next to your spouse) may prompt you to get out of the house and figure this retirement thing out.

Like I said, no easy answer. Think through the nature of your job and your spouse's job and your plans for retirement. Re-examine your projected financial requirements in retirement and your existing resources. Play out the thought experiment. If one of you retires early and the other doesn't, will you turn into Bill and Melinda (blush), or will your decision turn into a source of resentment? And one final pitch: If you get stuck, please, please, please go see a couples counselor. Getting help doesn't mean defeat. It means you're smart.

The Family Dynamic. While maintaining a strong relationship with a life partner should clearly be a priority, for many of us, there is a constellation of family members to consider as well. Many a parent is guilty of assuming that just because she is now retired, the kids will magically have time to come out and play. Before you fall into this trap and let the notion of spending more time with your children entice you into early retirement, give a little bit of thought to whether or not your children actually have the capacity to spend more time with you. If this section had an audio track, this is when *Cats in the Cradle* by Cat Stevens would start playing.

If you're contemplating retiring early, there is a healthy chance you worked exceptionally hard to accumulate enough wealth to make this life transition a real possibility. Are your kids doing the same thing as they launch careers of their own? Or are they entering the even more chaotic childrearing phase of life? In short, if hanging out with the kiddos is part of your retirement plan, ask yourself honestly—do they have time for you?

And before you pack up and move to a lovely home down the street from your kid, beware of the *grandparent childcare* conundrum. If your dream retirement involves changing the grandkids' diapers five days a week while your child grinds out long hours at work, I salute you. If, however, you fancy the occasional afternoon trip to the playground with your grandchildren, or maybe an outing to the ice cream shop once a week, please make sure you aren't sending the wrong message by relocating down the street from your child. As always, communication is critical. Avoid hurt feelings by getting very clear about your willingness to participate in childcare in your retirement years.

Finally, while purchasing a second home near your children (and/or grandchildren) might sound lovely, think carefully about whether or not this will be as idyllic as it sounds. If you plan to spend two weeks a year in your second home, and the rest of the year the home will be vacant, you might want to reconsider the purchase. From a financial planner's standpoint, this strategy rarely makes sense. Property tax and maintenance are often non-trivial, and while the home may indeed appreciate in value, keeping the sum required to purchase the home in a diversified investment account and instead plowing money back into the local economy by staying in a lovely hotel during the two weeks you plan to visit the kids might be a better bet.

The Great Thought Experiment. Now for the final project. If you are reading this book while continuing to work full-time, I want you to devote some time and energy to an interesting thought experiment. Imagine you have all the free time in the world. Yes, I know, this may be as foreign and unrelatable as asking you to contemplate what it feels like to walk on the moon. But really try. And now imagine what you will do with all that free time.

What is coming up? Are you already envisioning three years of touring the Americas in your luxury RV with your beloved spouse by your side, and is an ear-splitting grin already spreading across your beautiful face? Or are you imagining virtually exploring the world by devouring books in your cozy armchair in your rustic cabin on Orcas Island? Is the looming idea of retirement and the accompanying hours of free time terrifying, or is it liberating? Where do friends, family, and a sense of purpose fit into the retirement equation?

Now to the point: If this thought experiment is exhilarating and you feel like a kid who can't sleep because a trip to Disneyland is on the horizon, you may have your answer to the question of "Should I retire?" If you are sweating profusely and feeling something akin to vertigo, please don't make any dramatic changes until you've had a chance to further work through the question of whether or not retirement is the right move at this point in your life.

CHAPTER 2

Can I?

Whether or not you have enough to retire is contingent on several factors: (a) the total amount of financial assets you have accumulated, (b) the expected rate of return on those assets, (c) the income you will receive from other sources—e.g., social security, pensions, real estate rental income, (d) how long you will live, and (e) the amount you expect to spend in retirement. Let's start with the expense side of the equation and then move to income.

Budgeting

Ah, the manifold joys of budgeting (said no one ever). While I do encounter the occasional client who relishes tracking every dollar spent and who can recite with precision the standard deviation of his or her monthly net cash flow, most of my clients have yet to create a detailed budget for retirement. While maximizing retirement income is a topic I will address in detail later in this book, to answer the question of whether you can retire or not, you will first need to create a realistic budget. You will find a detailed sample budget in the appendix.

I suggest that you start this drill with an accurate current budget. This is a good starting point simply because you have access to the required information—i.e., you need not speculate. You can easily calculate exactly how much you are spending in an average month on housing costs, food, sundries, clothing, automobile expenses, insurance, medical expenses, entertainment, travel, and a host of additional costs by reviewing both your checking account activity and your credit card charges. Spend some time on this and get it right. If you've never created a budget before, the result can be sobering. *I never would have guessed that my stable of ponies and weekly private riding lessons at the Menlo Polo Club are the reason I am cash-flow negative, and perhaps purchasing that expensive time-share in Cabo San Lucas wasn't a great idea*!

Once you've accurately captured your current budget, we need to start speculating a bit. While we can never be certain exactly how much you might need to spend on living expenses in retirement, we can get pretty close with some hard work. Not surprisingly, the cost of clothing, food, travel, and entertainment varies quite a bit between individuals due to diverse lifestyles and spending habits. Simply do your best by analyzing your current budget and determining whether your expenses will change significantly in retirement.

As a general rule, most retirees require less monthly cash than they did during their working years. This is typically attributable to (a) a smaller tax bill—more on that later, and (b) no further need to save for retirement. Advisors will often cite 85 percent as a reasonable income replacement rate (meaning retirees will need to replace 85 percent of the income they earned during their working years), but this is too simpleminded to be particularly valuable. A few examples will highlight the issue.

On one extreme, a client who earned $1,000,000 per year (woo-hoo!) during her glory years at Google might only require $80,000 per year in retirement. Why? Seventy-five percent of her net earned income went into savings, which in turn allowed her to retire early, pay off her primary residence, and purchase her round-the-world sailboat with cash. Her frugal nature dictates that as she sails around the world, she will rent out her primary residence (making it cash-flow positive), and despite a never-ending list of boat repairs and those all-too-expensive slip fees in Europe, she only requires $80,000 pre-tax per year to live quite comfortably. Her income replacement rate (at the moment, anyway) is a meager 8 percent of her annual earned income prior to retirement.

On the other extreme, a client who earned $250,000 per year during his career as a primary care physician might require $300,000 per year in retirement. Why? He refinanced his primary mortgage note several times, and at age sixty, he is now into a new thirty-year fixed mortgage, so his housing costs are high. In addition, he wants to travel extensively (much more in retirement than during his working years), and he doesn't stay at the Motel 6, preferring the manicured lawns and rarefied air of the Four Seasons. His income replacement rate is a potentially worrisome 120 percent.

In short, creating a retirement budget is an important drill. As you put together your projections, four categories of expenses merit a closer look: housing expenses, medical expenses, emergency expenses, and the cost of caring for elderly parents.

Housing. Will your house be paid off by the time you retire? If so, do you plan to stay in the house, or do you anticipate moving to an area with a lower cost of living? As an advisor in the San Francisco Bay Area, I routinely watch clients flee the incredibly high cost of living in the region. If a client's house is still subject to a mortgage note, there is a good chance that she can sell the house and use the net proceeds to purchase a home outright in another state.

Does your home require a significant amount of maintenance? If so, and if you have historically done much of the work yourself, how long do you anticipate that you will be able to continue doing this work? Always allocate a reasonable amount to "maintenance and repair" when creating your budget. If you live in a well-insured condominium with an association that covers all external and common area repairs, a very modest budget of $100 per month may be more than adequate. If you live in a sprawling estate built in

1930 with suspect wiring and rickety plumbing, $500 per month may not be sufficient.

Think hard about property tax when you decide where you'll live in your retirement years. For clients in California, Proposition 13 is often an incredibly compelling reason to stay put. Proposition 13 effectively limits the increase in the taxable value of a home. Rather than face a property tax bill that grows in tandem with ever-increasing home valuations, homeowners in California are subject to a maximum increase in assessed value of 2 percent per year. The result has been that a Californian who purchased a home currently valued at $3,000,000 for $150,000 in the 1970s may pay less property tax than a pair of newlyweds who just purchased their first residence for $500,000. Significant public-policy issues aside, this can be a tremendously important factor when refining the housing element of a budget.

To take the Proposition 13 windfall a bit further, Californians over fifty-five years of age are able to move their artificially low property tax basis to another property. Due to the recent passage of Proposition 19—a detailed analysis of which is beyond the scope of this book—homeowners are able to transfer their property tax basis to another home up to three times. Notably, the new home can now be more valuable than the home sold, and a pro-rata calculation of the assessed value of the new home applies.

When refining the housing element of your budget, please carefully think through the topic of insurance. Far too many of my clients find that a very significant portion of their net worth is tied up in their primary residence. If you find yourself in a similar situation, make sure you have adequate homeowner's insurance (and in California, please obtain an earthquake policy as well). Flooding on the East Coast and wildfires on the West Coast have imparted a painful lesson on homeowners with "replacement cost" policies—

they haven't monitored the rise in the cost of construction in their area, and they find that the limit on the insurer's obligation to pay is too low, leaving them in a precarious situation.

Medical Expenses. Medical expenses represent a considerable portion of the average retiree's budget. Now, I realize that you aren't the average retiree, of course, but I still want you to devote some thought to how you will manage this non-trivial expense in retirement. Fidelity estimates that the average couple will need an astounding $295,000 (in today's dollars) to cover medical expenses in retirement.[i]

Unless you were a public employee (e.g., military, civil servant, etc.), it is unlikely that you will have access to employer-sponsored retiree health benefits. This is a sobering start to our analysis, and the news only gets worse. Indeed, the Kaiser Family Foundation reports that the average percentage of a household budget spent on health expenses is almost three times as much for retirees on Medicare as for working households (14 percent versus 5 percent).[ii] Finally, if you plan to retire before age sixty-five, the costs become even more daunting.

Now that I've injected an element of despair into the equation, let me lighten the mood a bit. If you are contemplating early retirement, it is likely that you have accumulated significant assets. Indeed, it is entirely possible that you may shrug at the notion that medical expenses for you and your spouse will rise well beyond $285,000 (depending on how early you retire). But even if you aren't among this lucky cohort of wealthy soon-to-be-early-retirees, one of the following options to bridge the gap between retirement and the start of Medicare may be manageable.

Remain on a Spouse's Employer-Sponsored Plan: In Chapter 1, I discussed the critical decision of whether you (and/or your spouse) *should* retire even if you *can* retire. If you elect to retire first and your spouse continues to work, you stand to save a considerable amount by remaining on your spouse's employer-sponsored plan.

COBRA Coverage: If your position was eliminated, and you are contemplating early retirement without the exuberance that can follow years of careful planning—i.e., you bought this book out of necessity—you may be eligible for eighteen months of COBRA coverage. COBRA is often relatively expensive, simply because you will be forced to pay not only 100 percent of what was previously deducted from your paycheck by your employer, but also 100 percent of the amount that your employer paid the insurer on your behalf for coverage. This is often eye-opening for clients who elect COBRA coverage for the first time. *But I only paid $250 per month for family coverage, and the same policy will be $1,950 per month going forward?* Yes, it sucks.

Private Market Plan: Of course, you can shop around for a private market health insurance plan. This offers you a great deal of flexibility, but the cost can be astounding. If you are fifty-five years old and you want to maintain halfway-decent health insurance in California, expect to pay north of $1,000 per month for coverage. Don't take my word for it, though. If you are contemplating retiring before Medicare kicks in, please, please, please obtain a few quotes for how much a health insurance policy will cost you and factor this amount into your budget.

As you approach age sixty-five, I suggest that you spend some time reviewing and considering all your Medicare options. A full-blown analysis of Medicare is not only beyond the scope of this book, but it would also bore you to tears. The good news: your monthly medical costs should drop considerably when you are eligible for Medicare. On that note, please do remember to sign up during your seven-month initial enrollment period that begins three months before the month you turn sixty-five.

If you are reading this book well before your target retirement date, I suggest that you explore the possibility of funding a health savings account (HSA). An HSA account is simply a mechanism for setting aside pre-tax dollars that you can use to pay out-of-pocket medical expenses. Funds in an HSA don't expire, and this makes an HSA a very attractive retirement planning vehicle. In 2020, you can contribute up to $3,550 per year to your HSA, and if you are age fifty or older, you can make an additional $1,000 annual contribution to your HSA.

In summary, I want you to brace yourself for sticker shock, do a fair amount of exploring, and come up with a very realistic estimate of both (a) the projected cost of your medical insurance premiums, both before and after age sixty-five, and (b) the projected cost of your out-of-pocket medical expenses, both before and after age sixty-five. The result of this tedious exercise will become a critical element of your retirement budget.

Emergency/Contingency Planning. Rather than allocate a portion of your monthly retirement budget to unforeseen emergency expenses, you should maintain an emergency cash reserve. Conventional wisdom among financial planners dictates that you retain the sum which equals six months of your monthly budget in a secure (FDIC-insured) savings account. For a middle-class couple in Oklahoma City, this might be $20,000. For a well-off couple in New York City, something closer to $200,000 might be reasonable. After completing your monthly projected retirement budget, you can multiply by six and then set aside the appropriate amount.

Caring for Elderly Parents. Many clients in their forties, fifties, and sixties find themselves uneasy members of the sandwich generation. After raising their own children and diligently saving like crazy for the ever-increasing cost of college, they accept responsibility for their own parents' financial well-being. For some clients, it's a no-brainer.

A former colleague was raised by a single father who immigrated from Vietnam in the 1970s with few prospects. He opened up his own shoe repair store, and by working ten hours each day, seven days a week, with nary a day off, he managed to keep his daughters fed and clothed, and he also somehow managed to spend enough time with his girls to imbue them with an acute sense of the value of an education. After graduating from both Stanford undergraduate and law schools, do you think the older daughter is committed to ensuring her dad enjoys retirement? You bet she is.

Conversely, a good friend was raised by a father who always commanded a very healthy income, but had a predilection for nice cars, fancy meals, and expensive vacations. He paid virtually no attention to his children, and he also contributed absolutely nothing to their education. When at age seventy-five he revealed that he was done working and hadn't accumulated a dime in retirement funds, do you think his children were interested in supplementing his social security paycheck? Not so much. A decade or two in a dilapidated double-wide near Death Valley builds character, after all.

Regardless of whether your parents were saint-like in their devotion to creating the model citizen that is clearly you, or whether they were seemingly unconcerned that you never bathed, attended school, or ate a square meal, you may find yourself supplementing their income in retirement. If you think that it is likely that they will require your financial assistance, begin planning for this eventuality sooner rather than later. Far too many families are hesitant to discuss financial affairs, and far too many parents are too proud to reveal to their own children that they are in financial distress. Do your best to create an open dialogue, and if they resolutely refuse to cooperate, well, there's always that double-wide near Death Valley. (Please just make sure that the place has air conditioning).

The cost of skilled nursing care has risen dramatically over the past few decades. In 2020, the average cost of a semi-private room in a skilled nursing facility in California is about $7,470 per month. Want a private room for a parent? Be prepared to pony up $8,669 per month. Keep in mind that the cost of a room varies geographically in a non-trivial way. A semi-private room in San Francisco will set you back an astounding $9,900 per month.[iii] If your parents are well-off or have diligently paid into a long-term care policy, they may be fine. If not, you may feel compelled to contribute to their income. Clearly the cost of five years ore more of skilled nursing care for a parent can set back a child's retirement plans by many years.

Sample Budget. To help guide you as you finish up the budgeting drill, I've created a sample monthly budget based on the needs of a couple in their early fifties contemplating retirement at age fifty-five in the very expensive San Francisco Bay Area. Let's name this couple Kevin and Diana Smith. The Smiths have two children who are out of college and largely (but not entirely) self-supporting. In addition, both Smiths are blessed with parents who are entirely capable of covering the costs of their own care in retirement. Diana is a sales executive at a technology company, and Kevin is a patent attorney at a mid-size firm. The Smiths own a home worth $2,000,000, have a nearly-paid-off mortgage note, and anticipate retiring in their current home.

Here is the Smith's budget:

Category of Expense	**Current Budget**	**Retirement Budget**
Housing:		
Mortgage Note	$3,000	$0
Property Tax	$1,000	$1,000
Homeowner's Insurance	$150	$150
Earthquake Insurance	$120	$120
Utilities (electricity, cable, internet, etc.)	$400	$400
Landscaping	$150	$150
Cleaning	$300	$300
Maintenance and Repair	$250	$400
Total Housing Expenses	*$5,350*	*$2,370*
Groceries and Sundries:	*$1,500*	*$1,500*
Automobile:		
Insurance and Registration	$150	$150
Gas	$400	$200
Maintenance and Repair	$100	$100
Total Automobile Expenses	*$650*	*$450*
Clothing:	$200	$200

Unreimbursed Medical & Dental Expenses:	*$100*	*$300*
*Medical Premium:**	*$300*	*$1,700*
Entertainment:	*$1,500*	*$1,500*
Travel:	*$1,000*	*$2,500*
Misc.	*$500*	*$500*
Support of Adult Children	*$500*	*$0*
Grand Total	***$10,420***	***$9,900***

* These figures assume that Diana has access to an employer-sponsored health insurance plan prior to retirement, and during the ten-year gap between retirement and age sixty-five (when Medicare kicks in), the Smiths will have to pay out-of-pocket for a health insurance policy.

Note that I have made several important assumptions about the Smiths: (1) they will pay off their mortgage note prior to retirement, (2) their children will have successfully "launched" prior to retirement, (3) their automobile expenses will decline due to no longer needing to commute to work, and (4) they plan to spend a fair amount of their free time during retirement traveling. All of this adds up to a retirement budget that isn't dramatically different from their budget while employed.

Income

I will explain how to best structure an investment portfolio to generate strong returns with limited volatility in Chapter 3. Then I will walk you through different withdrawal and income-generating strategies in Chapter 4. For the purposes of this chapter, however, let's keep the discussion fairly high-level and first analyze the basic question: *Am I Even Close*? To do that, we need to generalize quite a bit. (Yes, my accountant friends, you will have to suffer through the imprecision of this first chapter. We will speculate about future tax rates, make assumptions about investment returns, and otherwise avoid a detailed analysis. Sit tight—the stuff you love will come later.)

To get a rough handle on anticipated retirement income, we should first look at quasi-guaranteed sources of income. I use the term *quasi-guaranteed* because perfect security is a fiction, even with seemingly bulletproof defined benefit plans such as state and federal pensions. Said differently, let's first look at predictable sources of monthly income:

Pensions. Will you expect any pension payments in retirement? If so, count your lucky stars (or more appropriately, pat yourself on the back for having earned such a treasured asset). Examples of pensions are local and state pensions, military and civil service pensions, and corporate or private pensions. The latter are becoming quite rare. Pension payments naturally vary from the incredibly modest (a teacher with five years of service) to the very generous (a Kaiser Permanente physician with thirty years of service). To compare pension income (pre-tax) to expenses (post-tax), we'll have to make an assumption about tax rates in retirement.

Here's how it works: Pension payments are taxed at regular income tax rates. More specifically, while you will pay federal income tax and state income tax (if applicable) on your pension payments, you won't pay any Social Security tax or Medicare tax (known as "FICA") on the payments. Quick example: Let's suppose a couple in California with a single pension payment of $5,000 per month who files taxes jointly will pay approximately $745 per month in combined state and federal income tax. This couple would therefore use a monthly net pension income of $4,255 as a basis of comparison to their monthly expenses.

Annuities. An annuity is a contractual arrangement with an insurer to exchange an up-front premium for future guaranteed payments. Depending on the type of annuity purchased (qualified, or pre-tax v. non-qualified, or post-tax) the tax rules that apply to distributions can get a bit complicated. The basic idea: Imagine you use $100,000 in after-tax dollars to purchase a single-pay, lifetime annuity. As you receive payments in the future, your payments are pro-rated between your original investment (on which you've already paid income tax and therefore can't be taxed again) and earnings (which are taxable). This is done by applying what is called an exclusion ratio.

Like many financial advisors, I have a long-standing aversion to annuities that I will explain in much greater detail in Chapter 5. If you already purchased an annuity, don't fret about it—you may very well appreciate the stable income in retirement, and depending on how long you live, you may end up coming out on the right side of the annuity analysis.

Social Security Benefits. Social Security benefits are far more complicated than one would hope, and many a treatise has been written on how to best maximize your Social Security benefits in retirement. I examine Social Security in more detail in Chapter 4.

For our sanity, let's assume that you have enough additional taxable income in retirement (dividends, capital gains, 401(k) and IRA distributions, etc.) to ensure that you are taxed on 85 percent of your benefit, which is the maximum under the current applicable regulations. This means that 85 percent of your benefit is taxable at regular federal income tax rates. And no, you don't pay Social Security Tax or Medicare Tax (FICA) on your social security payments (though Medicare costs are deducted). Better yet, most states don't tax social security payments either. Normally, I have to deliver the bad news to Californians and New Yorkers, but in this case, only the following states tax social security according to the federal rule I just mentioned: Minnesota, North Dakota, Vermont, and West Virginia. A few additional states only partially tax social security: Colorado, Connecticut, Kansas, Missouri, Montana, Nebraska, New Mexico, Rhode Island, Utah. If your state isn't listed—Hallelujah—no state tax is payable on your social security benefit!

Now back to the task at hand—calculating net income for purposes of comparison to your monthly budget. Keep in mind that retiring early often has the unfortunate result of reducing your social security benefit. This is because your social security benefit is calculated based on your highest thirty-five years of income, and a big fat zero is inserted in your record for each year you didn't work. Regardless, let's keep it simple and work through another quick example. Imagine that a husband and wife in Arizona (no state income tax on social security payments), both of whom were strong earners for many years, receive a combined total of $7,000 per month in social security beginning at age seventy. Due to their other sources of income, let's assume that 85 percent of their Social Security benefit is taxable. If they file jointly, let's further suppose that the federal income tax payable on the $7,000 monthly payment is approximately $442. The net income they would use for purposes of comparison to their budget is therefore $6,558. Keep in mind that any income above and beyond their social security benefit will get taxed at a significantly higher rate due to the graduated nature of our income tax ladder. Here it is, in chart format:

Variable	Amount
(A) Total Social Security Benefit	$7,000
Taxable Social Security Benefit	$5,950
(B) Federal Tax Payable	$442
State Tax Payable	$0 (hooray!)
(C) Net Social Security Benefit (A - B)	$6,558

Now that we've walked through sources of quasi-guaranteed income, let's discuss income from retirement accounts and investment/brokerage accounts. I'll refer to both types of income generically as investment income.

Investment Income. We'll get to the issue of taxation of investment income later. First, however, we need to make a gross generalization about the return you can expect on retirement and investment accounts. By the time you finish reading Chapter 4, you'll have a very good idea of how probability applies to projections about investment income. A Monte Carlo simulation, which we will come back to in more detail in Chapter 4, is a sophisticated way to calculate the probability of a certain outcome. In other words, if we input assumptions about the total amount invested, average investment return, standard deviation (volatility), monthly spending, and life expectancy into Monte Carlo software, the resulting probability curve will show us whether or not we are likely to achieve our stated goal (which is often simply not outliving our assets).

Largely based on a 1998 paper titled *Retirement Savings: Choosing a Withdrawal Rate that is Sustainable*, often referred to as the Trinity Study, which was authored by three finance professors at Trinity University, financial planners have used the "Four Percent Rule" to crudely calculate how much can be withdrawn from an investment account each year over a long time horizon with an extremely small chance of running dry. The elementary school version of this analysis simply states that an individual has sufficient savings in assets for retirement if 4 percent of his or her assets are sufficient to cover a year's expenses. For reasons explained in much greater detail in Chapter 4, this rule is far from perfect. We will later "geek out" on the logic behind the rule, as well as the problems associated with the rule. For now, I'll simply ask you to take a big leap of faith and accept an assumed safe withdrawal of 3 percent for those who plan to retire in their fifties.

Now on to the issue of tax payable on investment income. Distributions from 401(k)s, IRAs, 403(b)s, 457s, and other tax-deferred accounts are always taxable at ordinary income tax rates. Because these distributions are not classified as earned income, Social Security Tax and Medicare Tax (FICA) are not payable on these amounts. Conversely, properly timed distributions from a Roth IRA are never taxable. Finally, the manner in which income from an investment account may be taxed varies a bit depending on how the income is categorized—options include long-term capital gains tax, short-term capital gains tax, qualified dividends, and non-qualified dividends.

Before your eyes gloss over (I see you nodding off), here is a table that puts it all together. The tax treatment descends from worst to best, and my standard disclaimer about generalizing a bit in the interest of the preservation of our sanity applies.

	Pre-Tax Retirement Accounts	Investment Accounts	Roth IRA Accounts
Regular Income Tax	✓		
Short-Term Capital Gains Tax (same as Income Tax)		✓	
Non-Qualified Dividends (same as Income Tax)		✓	
Long-Term Capital Gains Tax (preferential rates)		✓	
Qualified Dividends (same as Long-Term Capital Gains Tax)		✓	
No Tax on Distributions (if withdrawn properly)			✓

For reasons that aren't hard to surmise, when harvesting income from an investment account, we try for long-term capital gains tax treatment or qualified dividend tax treatment. Here's a quick example to help you decipher how calculating tax on investment income works. Imagine that a couple in California filing a joint return receives social security payments of $7,000 per month. On top of this, now imagine that the couple receives another $10,000 per month in combined long-term capital gains and qualified dividends.

Because social security payments are subtracted from the couple's gross income in their California return (thereby keeping state tax modest), let's imagine the state tax payable on the $10,000 per month in combined long-term capital gains and qualified dividends is $450 and the federal tax payable on the same $10,000 is $1,500. The net income on the $10,000 in investment income is therefore $8,050.

Putting It All Together

We now have the ingredients we need to crudely answer the key question: *Do I have enough*? To answer the question, we need to combine assumptions about (a) projected expenses in retirement, and (b) net income. To see how everything comes together, let's return to Diana and Kevin Smith, our fictional couple from the budgeting exercise we performed earlier. Here are the key assumptions we will use to decipher whether the Smiths are in a good position to retire early, or whether they should continue to remain employed for a few more years:

- The Smith's projected monthly budget in retirement is $9,900.

- The Smiths plan to defer on electing to receive their social security payments until age seventy (more on this strategy later). In other words, they will receive no payments during the first fifteen years of their retirement.

- The Smiths have no pensions and no annuities.

- The Smiths have a combined $2,000,000 in 401(k)s and pre-tax IRAs.
- The Smiths have $3,000,000 in an investment account.
- The Smiths have $80,000 in cash in an FDIC-insured savings account as an emergency reserve.
- The Smiths plan to withdraw 3 percent per year from their investment and retirement accounts, and they will likely accelerate this rate of withdrawal once they begin receiving social security payments.
- The Smiths will file joint federal and state income tax returns.

We've already sorted out the Smith's projected monthly retirement budget, so we need to focus on the net income side of their retirement equation. Here is the basic analysis, with tax implications very roughly estimated:

Step 1: *Calculate the Smith's gross income from retirement accounts and investment accounts.*

To do this, we simply multiply $5,000,000 by 3 percent, which is $150,000, or $12,500 per month.

Step 2: *Calculate the Smith's effective tax rate on this $12,500 per month.*

Accountants, hold your breath, as we are going to guesstimate a bit. Let's assume that the effective tax rate on this $12,500 per month (which is a combination of regular income tax on retirement account withdrawals and long-term capital gains tax on investment account withdrawals) is 5 percent for state tax and 7.5 percent for federal tax.

Total tax liability is therefore $12,500 x 12.5% = $1,562 per month, and net income is therefore $12,500 - $1,562 = $10,938 per month.

Step 3: *Subtract the Smith's projected net income from their projected expenses.*

$10,938 - $9,900 = $1,038 net positive cash flow per month.

Step 4: *Celebrate!*

The Smiths can most certainly retire early given that (a) a 3 percent return on the Smith's retirement and investment accounts exceeds their monthly budget, (b) the Smith's will have a substantial Social Security benefit beginning at age seventy, and (c) Medicare will significantly reduce the monthly cost of the Smith's medical premium at age sixty-five.

If in the future the Smiths decide that they want to gift their children money for significant expenses such as a wedding, a down-payment on a new residence, etc., they will have to carefully consider the impact such sizable cash outlays will have on their retirement plan. For now, though, the prognosis for an early retirement looks good.

What if It Doesn't Look Good?

For the sake of an easy example of a cash-flow problem, let's be pessimistic and change the monthly expense assumptions for the Smiths. Instead of $9,900 per month in projected monthly retirement expenses, the Smiths estimate that they will need $12,000 per month. As we calculated earlier, a 3 percent return on their retirement and investment assets yields a net income of $10,938. What now?

The Smiths have a few options, none of which are particularly desirable.

Option 1: *Reduce Expenses*

Well, duh, you may be thinking. Yes, it may seem quite obvious, but restraining spending in retirement is certainly an option for many. Do the Smiths really need that expensive country club membership? Or maybe their travel budget can be reduced from three nice vacations a year to two. If the Smiths can find approximately $1,100 to trim out of their monthly retirement budget, they should be fine.

Option 2: *Continue Working*

Another few years of working and saving may bridge the gap between projected income and projected expenses. If the Smiths are risk-averse and don't want to adjust their lifestyle expectations in retirement, a few more years of employment just might do the trick.

Option 3: *Use a Reverse Mortgage to Generate Additional Cash*

While I am not a fan of reverse mortgages in most instances, if bequeathing home equity to beneficiaries is not a priority, it is indeed possible to raid the home-equity piggy bank and use the proceeds to bridge a cash-flow shortfall. Note, however, that a borrower must generally be at least sixty-two years of age, and the amount that can be borrowed through a reverse mortgage is limited to the current FHA lending limit ($765,600 in 2020). In short, the Smiths are too young for this approach.

Option 4: *Increase the Withdrawal Rate from Retirement and Financial Accounts*

To analyze this properly, I need to remind you of the value of a Monte Carlo analysis, which can effectively capture the probability of running dry prior to death given any number of retirement scenarios. It comes down to risk tolerance. If instead of a 95 percent chance of success at a 3 percent withdrawal rate, the Smiths are willing to accept a 75 percent chance of success at a 4 percent withdrawal rate, they can simply adjust their withdrawal rate and hope for the best. At a 4 percent withdrawal rate, the increase in the Smith's net income is more than $3,000 per month —more than enough. The Smiths would likely work with the advisor to come up with the appropriate withdrawal rate between 3 percent and 4 percent to meet their budget. Perhaps 3.5 percent would be just right. If fate conspired against them and a cash infusion was required well into their retirement years, the Smiths could consider the reverse mortgage option described above.

Option 5: *Engage in Magical Thinking*

I'm kidding, of course. Don't do this. Relying on an annualized return of 20 percent per year on your investment account in retirement is as sensible as free diving with a great white shark. People have done both and survived, but don't expect to be among that cohort of lucky souls.

CHAPTER 3

How, Part I

Investing Intelligently

For those of you who find digesting financial concepts challenging, I am sorry to report that I am going to make you uncomfortable. It's good for you, I promise. Take your time getting through the ordeal. If you need to read some of the earlier sections of this chapter a few times to master the material, you're not alone. I often encounter clients who are apologetic about their lack of financial acumen. My response—*nonsense.* If we were all financial planners, the world would be an incredibly dull place.

For those of you who find investment theory interesting, this chapter may start at a level of detail that is too basic, but if I've done my job, you'll be nodding along and highlighting pithy nuggets of wisdom by the end. The point is that you should feel free to skip over what you already know. This chapter is intended as a progressive primer.

The Basics

<u>Risk and Return</u>

First, repeat after me. *Risk and return are related.*

If there is any single concept related to investing that I want you to understand, this is it. If anyone tries to peddle you an investment scheme that purports to deliver an incredible return with virtually no risk, run (don't walk) in the opposite direction. There is no such thing, my friend. Investments with a guaranteed high return and low risk simply do not exist. If you spend your free time searching for Nessie while diving in Lake Loch Ness or roaming the primeval forests of Washington State looking for Sasquatch, you have demonstrated a colorful affinity for magical thinking and the suspension of disbelief. When it comes to investing for retirement, I want you to flip off that little switch in your head. We need to get real.

Let's work through the sound logic underlying the risk/return relationship. First, we need to discuss the idea that investments are generally priced appropriately. If an investment offers a disproportionately high return for the amount of risk involved, guess what happens? Everyone jumps on that gravy train, and the price of the investment is driven up.

Free markets essentially work this way. Information about thousands of publicly traded stocks and bonds zips around the world at incredible speed and is quickly digested by investors, and the price of those stocks and bonds is continually refined to reflect the newly released information.

If the concept of risk v. return makes intuitive sense to you, you understand that if you stuff your investment portfolio chock full of incredibly safe investments (treasury bills are a good example), you are likely to receive a very modest return from your portfolio. However, the likelihood that you will end up suffering a significant loss is also exceptionally low. Conversely, if you invest in nothing but small-company international stocks, there is a chance you will hit a home run and laugh all the way to the bank, and there is also a chance that you will lose your shirt.

The two key elements of a generic investment portfolio are stocks and bonds. Stocks and bonds play different roles in a portfolio. Why? Because their risk profiles (and therefore expected returns) are quite different. To get a better handle on why this is the case, we need to explore the elements of risk that drive both stock returns and bond returns.

The Elements of Risk that Drive Stock Returns

First of all, for the newbies among us, let's quickly examine the fundamentals of holding stock as an investment. What is stock, after all? Stock (also referred to as "equity") is simply an ownership interest in a company. In other words, if you hold stock in a company, you own a piece of that company. It can all start to feel rather obscure, particularly when you own a share of a mutual fund or an index fund that in turn holds hundreds of stocks. At the end of the day, however, it is a relatively straightforward concept. By owning slices of various companies, you are investing in the innovation, efficiency, and hard work of the businesses that form the economic engine of our global economy.

Now on to the key components of risk that drive the return on various general categories of stock. I will refer to these general categories of stock as asset classes, and I'll start with the two basic differentiators.

Company Size. As a general rule, investing in large companies is considered less risky than investing in small companies, and for good reason. As a wealth manager in Silicon Valley, I watch with interest as small companies continually pop up, struggle mightily for a year or two, and then disappear. While these new companies are not publicly traded (i.e., the average Joe can't invest in them), they serve to illustrate a point. A small company with a single product in a constantly shifting marketplace is a much riskier investment than a larger company with a large cash reserve that enjoys a broadly diversified stream of revenue.

While large companies may be less risky, the likelihood that a well-established company will suddenly experience a meteoric increase in revenue is smaller than the likelihood that a small company will experience similar stupendous growth. Here's a somewhat ridiculous Godfather analogy that might appeal to those Francis Ford Coppola fans out there, with individuals in my analogy taking the place of publicly traded companies:

If you had a choice of investing in (a) Don Corleone himself, with his army of foot-soldiers and his healthy stream of revenue, or (b) an ambitious new upstart (let's call him Tony), who is a sly kid on the corner just starting to make a name for himself, which one is a safer bet? Don Corleone, of course. But while Don Corleone is a safer bet, he isn't likely to provide you with much of a return for investing in him. He's already a made man, after all. Conversely, the chances that Tony grows into a Corleone-like figure are small (i.e., he's a risky bet), but if he does become a made man, you should be rewarded handsomely for your investment.

Please don't take this as an endorsement of organized crime (which, despite what Hollywood would have us believe, generally isn't a good investment).

Value v. Growth. Investment managers and others in the finance world like to use the terms "value" and "growth" to describe two broad categories of stocks. In some ways, the descriptors are intuitive. Value must mean a stock is a good deal, right? And growth must mean a sock is going to grow like crazy, correct? Well, not necessarily. As you know by now, I don't mind generalizing, but let's make sure we get this right.

Value stocks are stocks that have a low price relative to various underlying accounting measures such as sales and earnings or book value. Think of value stocks as stocks with a black eye, a pronounced limp, a nervous tic. The term "value" is meant to indicate only that value stocks are currently priced modestly compared to other stocks with similar accounting measures. Will they provide you, the investor, with a good value? *Probably*. More on that later.

Growth stocks are stocks that have a high stock price relative to various underlying accounting measures. The subject companies are likely growing rapidly and may be highly profitable. Think of growth stocks as sexy stocks. The world is their playground, and many investors are drawn to them like paparazzi to a Kardashian.

Now that you understand the basic dimensions of risk that drive returns in the stock market, let's turn our attention to bonds.

<u>The Elements of Risk That Drive Returns in the Bond Market</u>

Just as we did for stocks, let's first define a bond (also referred to as "fixed income"). Simply put, a bond is a loan.

More precisely, a bond is a loan to an entity (such as a corporation, a state, or the United States government) that typically involves interest payments delivered at regular intervals to the creditor/bondholder, with the principal amount of the loan payable on a specific due date (known as the maturity date). Bonds are traded both in public markets and in private exchanges between brokers and creditors. Accordingly, the price of a bond (the amount someone is willing to pay for the bond) rises and falls until the bond reaches maturity.

Bonds are not terribly sexy, and they are included as an element of a standard investment strategy in no small part because they dampen the overall volatility of a portfolio. I'll dive into this concept of blending stocks and bonds in a portfolio in great deal later in this chapter.

For now, just as we did for stocks, let's examine the factors that govern risk and return with bonds. Bonds are often less risky investments than stocks, with some notable exceptions, of course (junk bonds, anyone?). The amount of interest an investor expects to collect on a loan to a company or government entity (remember, a bond is a loan) varies according to the following risk factors:

Credit Risk. So you thought that lending money to Dewey, Cheatum, and Howe, Inc. was a winning prospect and that the 10 percent interest on the bond was entirely reasonable? Sadly, you were wrong. DCW went into insolvency, and you've lost your entire investment. This is an extreme example of credit risk. If a company's credit is downgraded and you decide to sell your bond, you will receive a lesser amount for the bond. This is a less severe example of credit risk. Remember, however, that absent default, you will receive your investment back if you hold a bond until maturity.

Why is the return on United States Treasury Bills so paltry in comparison to corporate bonds? Credit risk, of course. Would you feel more secure lending money to Dewey, Cheatum, and Howe, Inc. or to a government that has never defaulted on a bond obligation? No points for getting this one right—too easy. If you got it wrong, well… my condolences. It's going to be a long road.

Maturity Risk. Life in the ultra-competitive business world is tough. No matter how sparkly the reputation of a particular bond issuer, the longer you, the bondholder, have to wait to get your investment back, the riskier the bond. Stuff happens. A company's credit may be downgraded, the municipality could go bankrupt. If you have to wait longer to collect, you expect a bit more. Got it?

Maturity risk certainly applies to corporate bonds, but it is not a significant risk factor for treasury bonds. This is simply because while corporations do indeed default on their bond obligations, the federal government has never done so.

Inflation Risk. Quickly now: What is inflation? Inflation is an increase in the price of goods or the weakening of the purchasing power of a dollar. Here is an example to illustrate the point. Imagine you are obsessed with Big Macs. Today you can buy ten Big Macs for ten dollars, and two years from now, you can only get six Big Macs for ten dollars. Presuming the prices of other goods rise in tandem with Big Macs, we can assume that this is inflation at work.

And why do bondholders care about inflation? They care because inflation erodes real returns, and real returns (inflation-adjusted returns) are more important than nominal returns (the interest payable). If I promise to pay you 5 percent per year for lending me money, but the price of your treasured Big Mac is rising at 6 percent per year, your real return is -1 percent per year.

We've grown somewhat complacent about inflation. If you don't remember the double-digit inflation of the 1970s, either (a) you're on the young side for early retirement—good for you!—or (b) this book has withstood the test of time and is still selling many years after initial publication. Either way, my point is that low inflation rates are not a given. Inflation risk is real, and it is something bond holders spend a great deal of time analyzing.

Volatility

It's critical that you grasp the concept of volatility in financial markets and understand why: (a) volatility is scary, and (b) it isn't. Say what? To fully understand volatility, which translates into risk, we first need to explore how volatility is measured. The standard measure of volatility among investment advisors is known as *standard deviation*, which is simply the statistical measure of the degree to which a series of returns of a particular investment differs from the average return of that same investment. About two-thirds of the time a return will fall within one standard deviation of the average.

Here are two examples to clarify what I mean:

The Snooze-Fest Fund. Shares of Snooze Fest mutual fund have an expected average annual return of 4 percent and an expected standard deviation of 2 percent. About two-thirds of the time, shares of Snooze Fest will produce an annual return of between 2 percent and 6 percent (i.e., the average return, plus or minus two percent). This range of results is referred to as one standard deviation.

The Heart Attack Fund. Shares of Heart Attack mutual fund have an expected average annual return of 12 percent and an expected standard deviation of 30 percent. Quick reminder: If standard deviation is 30 percent upward or downward, "one standard deviation" encompasses an eye-popping range of 60 percent. Therefore about two-thirds of the time shares of Heart Attack will produce an annual return of between 42 percent and -18 percent (i.e., the average return, plus or minus 30 percent).

Heart Attack is clearly a risky investment, while Snooze Fest is a much more secure investment. That being said, the average annual return of Heart Attack is quite a bit higher (12 percent) than the average annual return of Snooze Fest (4 percent). So you should always prefer to invest in Heart Attack, right? Not necessarily.

High standard deviation has two substantial negative impacts on a portfolio: (1) the rule of compounding returns ensures that the bad years that eventually go hand-in-hand with high standard deviation hurt very badly indeed, and (2) if an investor is forced to withdraw funds after a year of particularly dismal returns, this problem is exacerbated even further.

First, let's examine the concept of compounding returns. One way to digest the concept is to understand that this year's annual return creates a new principal amount for the growth or decline of the investment next year. Let's start with a very basic example that doesn't relate to investing in the stock market. Instead, we'll look at an investment with a guaranteed positive return, like a savings account.

For our example, imagine you hold $100,000 in a traditional savings account that pays you interest at an annualized rate of 2 percent. Now we'll examine how compounding interest compares to interest that doesn't compound.

Compounding Interest

Year	Growth of $100,000
1	$102,000
2	$104,040
3	$106,121
4	$108,243
5	$110,408

Non-Compounding Interest

Year	Growth of $100,000
1	$102,000
2	$104,000
3	$106,000
4	$108,000
5	$110,000

At the end of Year 5, the difference in the savings account balance ($408) isn't terribly exciting, is it? This is simply because the interest rate is modest. But to get your blood pumping, let's look at a compound interest rate of 10 percent on an initial investment of $100,000. Warning: To achieve a 10 percent return each and every year like clockwork in the stock market isn't possible absent fraudulent behavior (think "Ponzi scheme").

Compounding Interest

Year	Growth of $100,000
1	$110,000
2	$121,000
3	$133,100
4	$146,410
5	$161,051

Non-Compounding Interest

Year	Growth of $100,000
1	$110,000
2	$120,000
3	$130,000
4	$140,000
5	$150,000

This time the difference in the savings account balance ($11,051) is substantial and illustrates why Warren Buffet gets excited about compound interest. To quote him directly, "My wealth has come from a combination of living in America, some lucky genes, and compound interest."

Now that we've made it through the easy stuff, we need to take a closer look at our old foe, volatility (i.e., standard deviation). Investing in the stock market has never consistently produced positive annual returns for a long series of years, and we are deluding ourselves if we think that it ever will. So what happens when those painful years of negative annual returns arrive? In short, the concept of compounding interest works in reverse. A stock portfolio that is worth $100,000 and suffers a 50 percent loss in Year 1 (reducing the portfolio to $50,000) needs a positive return of 100 percent in Year 2 to get back to $100,000. Yikes! Thank goodness a well-diversified portfolio doesn't experience this kind of volatility.

To illustrate the problem in a more granular way, let's compare two portfolios with the same average return, but with different standard deviations. Once again we'll assume an initial investment of $100,000 and a five-year time horizon. Both portfolios will have an average annual return of 7 percent, but Mello Folio will have a standard deviation of 3.2 percent, while Jumpy Folio will have a standard deviation of 19.6 percent.

Mellow Folio

Year	Growth of $100,000	Annual Return
1	$105,000	5.0%
2	$111,300	6.0%
3	$115,752	4.0%
4	$129,642	12.0%
5	$140,014	8.0%

Jumpy Folio

Year	Growth of $100,000	Annual Return
1	$116,000	16.0%
2	$96,280	-17.0%
3	$127,090	32.0%
4	$116,922	-8.0%
5	$130,953	12.0%

	Mellow Folio	Jumpy Folio
Average Return	**7.0%**	**7.0%**
Compound Return	**7.0%**	**5.5%**
Standard Deviation	**3.2%**	**19.6%**

Jumpy Folio, despite enjoying the same average return as Mellow Folio, winds up with $9,061 less at the end of only five years (i.e., it has a lower compound return). This significant difference is driven by the impact of volatility. After this exercise, I hope you now better understand why we can't just focus on average return when selecting investments for a portfolio. Standard deviation is also critically important.

So what's the Holy Grail of investments? Something that produces a very high average return with a very low standard deviation. Remember, we are keeping it real (no magical thinking here), so instead of expecting the Holy Grail to materialize, later in this chapter we will explore how you can layer various investments inside a portfolio to maximize return and minimize standard deviation.

Okay, okay, you're thinking, I now understand why volatility (and its measure, standard deviation) is so important. Sadly, we're not done yet. I noted earlier that if an investor needs to withdraw funds at a low point in the market, the problem of volatility is further exacerbated. Keep in mind that periodically withdrawing funds from an investment account is exactly what we do in retirement.

To illustrate this issue, let's use exactly the same scenario as before, with one simple modification. Let's imagine that you need to withdraw $3,000 annually from your portfolio. What happens to the account balances at the end of Year 5? I'll spare you another table and cut to the chase. The Mellow Folio balance at the end of Year 5 is 21.0 percent lower than the previous scenario because of the withdrawals, and the Jumpy Folio balance at the end of Year 5 is 21.5 percent lower.

This is not an earth-shattering difference, but it has some impact. Let's now imagine that instead of periodic withdrawals, you are forced to withdraw a single lump sum of $40,000 from the portfolio at the end of Year 2 to address an emergency. The Mellow Folio balance at the end of Year 5 is 36 percent lower than our original scenario because of the emergency withdrawal, while the Jumpy Folio balance at the end of Year 5 is 42 percent lower.

The take-away: The additional impact of volatility on a portfolio when regular and sensibly modest withdrawals are taken is not catastrophic, but the additional impact of volatility on a portfolio when a large sum is withdrawn at exactly the wrong time is painful indeed.

Congratulations! You're now ready to take what you've learned about risk and return and the role of standard deviation and apply it to building an investment portfolio that should carry you safely through your retirement years. To do that, let's first explore the key decisions you will need to make.

Stocks v. Bonds

Later in this chapter I will address additional asset classes such as real estate, commodities, life insurance, and annuities. At this point, however, we should start by addressing the basic building blocks of any investment portfolio—namely, stocks and bonds. Stocks generally carry a higher risk and a higher average return, while bonds generally carry a lower risk and a lower average return. Stocks are the engine in your portfolio and short-term bonds are the airbag. In other words, you can zip around town without an airbag, but in the event of a crash, that airbag just might preserve that beautiful mug of yours.

In earlier examples we explored the impact of volatility on a portfolio and analyzed the additional impact of the timing of withdrawals. Now we can get more practical and focus on both your needs in retirement and how your personality should shape your investment strategy. To simplify the discussion a bit, we'll focus on several different factors that might influence your risk tolerance and therefore dictate your stock/bond allocation: (a) the number of years until you need to start taking withdrawals from your portfolio (I'll call this your "time horizon"), (b) your psychological tolerance for risk, (c) the existence of other sources of income, and (d) the amount of investment income you require to live comfortably in retirement.

Risk Tolerance (the Time Horizon Factor). If you are an overachiever and reading this book at age thirty-five, first of all, I commend you for your foresight. You get an A+ on your report card and a shiny new pocket protector. If you like the idea of retiring at fifty-five, you have a twenty-year time horizon. Twenty years is long enough that you can afford to take substantial risk. You still have many years of earnings ahead of you, which in turn means you have a greater capacity to accelerate your portfolio's recovery from poor market returns by infusing more capital into your investment account. If the worst happens and your portfolio's return is truly dismal, you may be able to defer retirement a few extra years and tough it out prior to taking withdrawals from your account.

If you are reading this book at age fifty-five, and tomorrow is your last day of work, well, better late than never. You get a B on your report card (because most people do absolutely no planning). Unlike your thirty-five-year-old self, you may need to start taking distributions from your investment account immediately, and once you're out of the workforce, the odds that you can soften a painful market downturn by re-entering the workforce diminish with each passing year. (This is true unless you are an aspiring Walmart greeter. Walmart greeters present a nice counterpoint to the age discrimination in Silicon Valley I noted earlier).

Are you trying to get rich, or stay rich? If you are thirty-five, you're likely entering your juiciest years of wealth accumulation. If you're fifty-five and thinking about retirement, you may be trying to stay rich. Getting rich involves working hard and taking risks (or inheriting money), while staying rich involves limiting risk and controlling spending.

Risk Tolerance (the Psychological Factor). I just insinuated that if you are thirty-five, your time horizon *may* prompt you to accept more risk. Conversely, if you are fifty-five, your time horizon *may* prompt you to tolerate less risk. This sounds rational enough, but the issue of risk tolerance is much more complex than that. Why? Human psychology is at play, and no Excel spreadsheet will explain how we think. Remember, I want you to live a joyful life, so how you *feel* about investing should have an impact on your strategy.

Are you already sitting on your lotus flower, eyes closed, contented smile on your face, while constantly changing stock prices buzz around your head like a cloud of angry hornets? If so, congratulations! You are either incredibly checked out or incredibly evolved. Either way, it's a good thing. Let me explain.

One of the most acclaimed books on the topic of meditation is titled *Zen Mind, Beginner's Mind*, and it's a compilation of the teachings of the late Zen master Shunryu Suzuki. The title of the book itself is telling. Students who meditate for the first time often have a powerful experience. This is because a beginner's mind is open, curious, and unbound by concepts and opinions. Once the study of meditation begins in earnest, monkey mind (the distracting internal voice that makes meditating extremely difficult) rears its irritating little head. Only after a great deal of effort can most practitioners make it back to the openness of a beginner's mind.

When it comes to investing, monkey mind is the anxiety that comes from paying too much attention to the movement of capital markets. It is truly crazy-making for many. A client who has never paid attention to the financial press, doesn't know (or even cares to know) how financial markets work, and is open and willing to accept advice from a competent planner is a good example of beginner's mind at work. Conversely, a client who doesn't have a strong grasp of how markets work, but carefully studies every spam-a-licious article titled, "Investor Who Made Billions Says Sell Everything Now!" is a nice example of monkey mind at work. Finally, a seasoned investment advisor may be an example of someone who started with beginner's mind, spent many years suffering through the fingernail-chewing effects of monkey mind, and finally climbed back onto that lotus flower.

An investor with beginner's mind may respond to a severe market downturn with a yawn. She will simply trust her advisor's advice to stay the course and wait for the market to recover. An investor with monkey mind may respond to a severe market downturn by succumbing to panic and selling at exactly the wrong time. A good advisor will acknowledge the short-term pain, then quickly set it aside and allow the present discomfort to fall into its rightful place in a long continuum of market movements.

I'll get to the point. While daily fluctuations in market prices don't rattle the minds of seasoned advisors or newbies who simply don't pay attention to the financial press, many investors have a very hard time tolerating the constant fluctuation of stock market returns.

If you can't help but check your portfolio balance six times a day, you may want to accept less risk in your portfolio for your mental and emotional well-being. As humans, we are perfectly primed to invest poorly (sell low, buy high), and I don't want you to fall into this trap. Increasing the allocation of bonds in your portfolio will reduce volatility and smooth out the return curve a bit. While I can bury you in information about the probability of a positive investment result, or the superior returns provided by stocks as compared to bonds over a long time horizon, and/or a myriad of other rational justifications for adjusting your portfolio, I will never discount the value of sleeping soundly at night. What's the use of accumulating additional wealth if it comes at the expense of an ulcer and insomnia?

You're not an android, or you wouldn't be reading this book. There are more detailed treatises on investing that aren't saturated with my goofy sense of humor, after all. But presuming for a moment that you aren't an android, the table below is a useful way of determining the right blend of stocks and less volatile assets (such as short-term, high-quality bonds). The chart suggests a maximum stock allocation for various risk tolerance levels (measured as a maximum acceptable percentage loss in a portfolio).

Maximum Acceptable Loss (%)	Maximum Stock Allocation (%)
10	10
15	20
20	30
25	40
30	50
40	60
45	70
50	80
55	90
60	100

Now that we've touched on both the time horizon element of risk tolerance and the psychological element of risk tolerance, we need to examine how your other sources of available income (if any) might impact your risk tolerance.

Risk Tolerance and the "Other Sources of Income" Factor. To understand why other stable sources of income in retirement might increase your tolerance for risk, let's work through a real-world example.

Susan is a divorced, sixty-year-old, recently retired elementary school teacher whose father both wrote and sang a catchy Christmas jingle that airs non-stop each December. In addition to a teacher's pension of $4,000 per month, Susan receives approximately $2,000 per month in royalty payments from her father's estate. Susan's house is paid off, and she is in good health. Her kids are out of college and don't need her financial help, and she holds approximately $1,200,000 in an investment account.

Working with her financial advisor, Susan determines that a $6,000 monthly budget will accommodate her passion for fine food and frequent vacations. After taking taxes into consideration (remember, that $6,000 in combined pension payments and royalties she receives is taxable), her advisor calculates that Susan will need to withdraw 1 percent of her portfolio each year to meet her needs. Susan is quite content with her life. However, she dreams big, and her number one priority beyond enjoying retirement is to donate enough to her church to allow the congregation to build a sparkling new parish hall. The projected cost is $4,000,000.

Susan could easily survive on her existing sources of income if necessary. Her teacher's pension is an unusually secure source of income, and her royalty payments have been consistent for many years (and are totally uncorrelated with market returns). Skipping that semi-annual trip to the Napa Valley wine country and downgrading from a balcony cabin to an interior cabin on that next cruise might be enough to survive on her pension and royalties alone. If her portfolio takes a big hit, Susan is in a good position to withstand the blow. And what about her dream of donating enough to her church for that new parish hall? Well, to achieve that long-standing goal, she's going to need a very healthy return on her portfolio, particularly if the costs of construction in her hometown continue to climb.

After discussing her goals with her advisor, Susan decides to go for a home run. She ratchets up the equity allocation in her portfolio to 80 percent (much higher than typically recommended for clients in retirement). She knows that her portfolio could potentially take a painful beating in any given year, and she is comfortable with the risk involved. As a former elementary school teacher, not much rattles Susan. She hopes that at age eighty she will be able to hand an enormous check to her church with a big smile on her face, but if she ends up having significantly less to leave behind when she eventually passes away, she knows the church will be delighted with whatever she leaves them.

The moral of the story? A public pension is the epitome of stability, and it frees up an investor like Susan to consider a more aggressive investment strategy if either (a) a higher return is needed to achieve the investor's desired standard of living, (b) the investor wants to leave beneficiaries a significantly larger estate, or (c) like Susan, the investor has an ambitious plan that will ultimately require a large pool of capital.

The *Other Sources of Income Factor* can also work in reverse in the years prior to retirement, depending on the nature of the income itself. To understand why, consider this example:

Daniel is a very successful venture capitalist. By helping match investors with early-stage companies (i.e., extremely high-risk/high-reward startups), he has accumulated many millions in savings and investments. He also has a significant carried interest in the fund he manages. Where would you peg Daniel's risk tolerance with respect to his personal investments?

If you yelled out "high!" because he's a venture capitalist, and his uber-dangerous funds have produced negative returns for investors more often than not (so of course he doesn't mind risk), we have some work to do. As my favorite professor in the Stanford history department used to say with a mischievous grin, "Very interesting. There is only one small problem with your theory. It's *wrong*."

Daniel's no dummy, you see. He will readily acknowledge that his venture funds rarely produce a positive return. Nonetheless, he still gets paid handsomely for his work. Daniel's predictable monthly income derived from managing the funds is more than adequate to cover his bills. In those rare years during which his funds do produce a positive return, Daniel's carried interest is tremendously valuable.

Now I will find out if you were paying attention earlier when we discussed the components of risk that drive stock returns. If you were to generically classify investments in startups using the key components of risk, how would you do it? One of the classifications is easy, company size (remember big is usually safer than small). Brand-new startups are typically small. Very, very small. So small, in fact, that the thought of a public listing is a distant thought.

What about the other dimension of risk? Remember, growth stocks are cute, while value stocks have ugly mugs. Accordingly, brand-new startups can't be value stocks. They have no track record. Instead, these adorable little companies are nothing but raw ambition. Think of them as sea turtle hatchlings. Have you ever seen an ugly sea turtle hatchling? Everyone loves them (so *cute*), but their odds of successfully growing into a majestic adult are extraordinarily low. Those seagulls are insatiable. You get the idea. Investors purchase interests in startup companies for their growth potential alone.

Now back to Daniel. His carried interest in his venture fund offers him outsized exposure to small, growth stocks, which is a high-risk, high-reward market segment. Accordingly, Daniel asks his investment advisor to structure his portfolio in a very conservative fashion—i.e., heavy on short-term bonds and large-cap stocks. Said differently, Daniel intelligently folds his work-related exposure to risky investments into his strategy for managing his own investment portfolio.

Risk Tolerance (the "How Much Risk Do I Need to Take" Factor). Perhaps daily market movements give you jitters. Perhaps every time the financial media loudly proclaims that the sky is falling (which is daily), you pour yourself a big shot of whiskey and start re-organizing your bugout bag. *Hunting rifle, check, compass, check, gold bullion, check, water purifier, check, flamethrower for defending against the zombie hordes, check.*

Here's the point: If you are terrified of capital markets, but you just *feel* like investing in stock is the right thing to do, I want you to stop and challenge this feeling. Do you need a big return? Maybe you will be just fine if your portfolio simply keeps up with inflation, or at worst, very slowly declines in value. If you ran through the budget drill earlier in this book and came up with $14,000 per month, and then you did a back-of-the napkin calculation of your required withdrawal rate from your $40M portfolio (wouldn't that be nice?) and came up with 0.05 percent (or $20,000) per month, maybe this whole stock market magic carpet ride isn't for you.

Economists like to use fancy terminology for basic concepts. *Marginal utility* is a term that describes how much benefit or satisfaction you get from consuming an additional unit of a good or service. We can take this concept and apply it to money. Sometimes money has a high personal marginal utility (i.e., each additional dollar has a profound impact on your lifestyle), and sometimes it has a low marginal utility (i.e., you already live like a 19th-century oil baron and can't imagine why you would want to increase your spending).

When determining your appetite for risk, I suggest that you examine your retirement budget and ask yourself: *Would a larger return really change my lifestyle in a significant manner?* If the answer is yes, perhaps a higher appetite for risk is sensible, and if the answer is no, perhaps you can ratchet back the risk in your portfolio.

Whether or not you feel compelled to leave behind a significant estate for your loved ones may not only impact (a) your withdrawal rate, but also (b) your tolerance for risk inside your portfolio. Leaving behind highly appreciated assets for beneficiaries is currently a winning strategy under the Federal Tax Code. This is because beneficiaries generally receive a step-up in tax basis when the owner of the appreciated assets dies. Said more simply, after your death, your beneficiaries may be able to sell shares of stock without any tax implications that would have otherwise triggered a massive capital gain. Accordingly, if you are particularly committed to leaving behind a significant estate for the benefit of your loved ones, both of the following factors may increase your appetite for risk: (a) the desire to obtain robust growth in your portfolio up until the date of your death, and (b) the tax benefit of leaving behind appreciated stock.

There is a reason I have dwelled on the concept of risk tolerance. Your appetite for risk determines how much of your portfolio you should allocate to bonds v. stocks. Let's imagine you've sorted this out. Based on extensive discussion with your advisor, you've determined that a 60/40 blend of stocks and bonds feels just right. What next? First, let me congratulate you on taking a significant first step toward creating a sensible portfolio. This is great progress. Alas, there is still much to learn. We will next turn to the actual mechanics of creating that perfect portfolio.

How to Diversify

If you're paying attention, you may have noticed that I titled this subsection "How to Diversify," rather than "Whether to Diversify." I am jumping headfirst into the issue of how to diversify assets in a portfolio because you are already advanced enough to recognize why diversification matters. Remember that persistent old foe, volatility, and its measure, standard deviation? Volatility not only makes our monkey minds howl in protest, but it also negatively impacts the compound return of a portfolio.

We spent a great deal of time working through the stock v. bonds allocation, which does indeed represent a high-level (and critical) form of diversification. Now let's briefly examine the benefits of further diversification within each category.

Stock Diversification. Remember the late 1990s? Of course you do. If your experience was like mine, you may have watched as your friends initially grew wealthy by investing heavily in technology stocks. You may have also watched with some concern (you are an empathetic person, after all) as their butts were handed to them when the technology sector imploded. While any broad market index took a beating in 2000, your friends who were invested solely in technology stocks didn't just receive a black eye, they suffered two black eyes, three broken ribs, and a busted lip.

What was the problem? Your friends were invested in many different technology stocks, after all. While this was better than the alternative of holding only one technology stock, they learned the hard way that whole market sectors can decline. In other words, they figured out the micro part (don't invest solely in Cisco), but they missed the macro part (whole sectors can get clobbered).

The negative implications of failing to diversify holdings within a portfolio are bad enough, but I have increasingly been alarmed with the resurgence of the "double-down" approach in the San Francisco Bay Area. I see this most often with clients who were too young to fully appreciate the tech crash in 2000. The double-down approach involves an employee holding nothing other than the stock of his employer inside an investment account. If the employer's stock price tumbles for any reason, the employee may not only lose much of his net worth, but also his job.

A very real example of the double-down approach is a Facebook employee with a deliciously high income whose entire net worth (roughly $5,000,000) was held entirely in shares of Facebook. Initially, this tech samurai didn't understand why beads of sweat were popping up on my forehead and my left eye was twitching. After all, holding nothing but Facebook shares had produced stupendous returns for this gentleman for years. Wouldn't the joyride continue forever? I told him that I visualized him standing atop a ten-meter platform, arms raised high in preparation for a perfect swan dive into an empty swimming pool. Happily, this client had an odd sense of humor, and it wasn't the end of our conversation. He got the point.

Different assets can either be positively correlated (the returns of the assets tend to move up and down from their average returns at roughly the same time), negatively correlated (the returns of the assets tend to move up and down from their average returns at different times), or uncorrelated (the returns of the assets move from their average returns at unrelated times). Including assets that are negatively correlated or at least uncorrelated reduces the standard deviation of a portfolio. Quick test: Is reducing the standard deviation of a portfolio a good thing? If you answered yes, congratulations on remembering the *only* critical lesson in the volatility chapter. If you answered no, please write *High Standard Deviation is Bad* on the blackboard fifty times in your neatest handwriting. Here is the basic idea in table format:

Volatility
Low standard deviation is good!
High standard deviation is bad!

Asset Correlation
Positive correlation = the assets being compared tend to deviate from their mean (average) returns in both positive and negative directions at the same time.
Negative correlation = the assets being compared tend to deviate from their mean (average) returns in both positive and negative directions at different times.

Correlation is more confusing than one would hope. Many financial advisors (including yours truly) and even academics in the field initially get this wrong. A full description of what correlation truly entails—i.e., the timing of deviation from mean returns, rather than simply movements in asset price—is beyond the scope of this book. Just understand that there actually aren't a huge number of examples of stock sectors that are negatively correlated. That being said, the returns of oil and gas stocks and airline stocks tend to move in opposite directions for a straightforward reason. Oil companies tend to prefer high oil prices (duh), while airlines tend to prefer low oil prices (makes sense, as fuel is one of an airline's biggest expenses).

While the correlation between international stock markets and domestic stock markets does vary significantly over time, including international stocks in a portfolio is an intelligent choice. This is not only because international stocks can provide investors with generous returns in good years, but also because there is often a non-trivial diversification benefit that comes with holding international stocks.

The concept of correlation brings up an important psychological principle that I want you to embrace. Remember monkey mind and beginner's mind? Please take a breath, close your eyes, and don't fret over the short-term movement of the various market sectors within your portfolio. Instead, periodically (but not daily, or even weekly) monitor your overall portfolio performance. Selling every stock in a market sector that has been stagnant for years might feel like the right choice in the heat of the moment, while doubling down on investments that have done particularly well might also feel sensible. Don't do it. Fight your human frailty and sit tight.

Bond Diversification. Remember, bonds are fundamentally quite different than stocks. They are essentially loans. Diversifying bond holdings is therefore a different exercise from diversifying stock holdings, and certainly less of a concern in many instances. While some investment advisors feel differently, I do not believe that the risk/reward ratio of high-yield bonds ("junk bonds") is sensible. Accordingly, my clients typically tolerate reasonable risk on the stock side of the equation, and very little risk on the bond side of the equation. If you insist on holding high-yield bonds (yuck), you should diversify the substantial risk involved by investing across a number of different market segments and geographies.

If all of your bonds are short-term treasuries, you aren't really exposed to any credit risk (the U.S. government had *better not* default) and you have minimal maturity and inflation risk (these are short-term bonds, after all). Further, the standard deviation of treasuries is extraordinarily low, so diversifying your bond holdings may not be a big issue.

If you are a fan of municipal bonds (likely due to the tax-free income they produce), you should know that while the standard deviation of municipal bond fund returns is fairly low, and the likelihood of a default by a municipality is extraordinarily low, defaults do happen. As a result, consider investing in a fund that holds many different municipal bonds to mitigate your risk.

Rebalancing

Over time, the allocation of asset classes inside your portfolio will drift. This is simply the natural result of one asset class outperforming the other. As your asset allocation drifts, your exposure to risk will also shift. For example, if it was a banner year for emerging market stocks, this asset class will grow into an outsized position in your portfolio, and you may find yourself with a portfolio that exceeds your tolerable level of volatility/risk. Conversely, if it was a terrible year for stocks and therefore the bonds in your portfolio outperform (this does indeed happen), you may find yourself with a portfolio that is heavy on bonds and has lower volatility (which is nice), but less capacity to produce a strong annual return (not so nice).

Often rebalancing has a relatively modest impact on a portfolio, and it will not always enhance the return of a portfolio (a common myth among investment advisors). Nonetheless, it keeps your portfolio in alignment with your original assessment of your tolerable level of risk/volatility, and it provides a nice means of exercising some discipline in your approach to investing.

There are various ways to manage the process of rebalancing a portfolio. One approach we can immediately dismiss is rebalancing at defined short intervals of time (i.e., daily, weekly, or even monthly) and automatically trimming back each and every position that has grown beyond its initial target percentage of your portfolio. Why is that bad? This would create way too much churn inside your portfolio. Trading cost and capital gains implications will start to erode your real return.

A more sensible approach to rebalancing is to create a rule governing the minimum and maximum amount each asset class allocation will be allowed to drift. There is no perfect rule here (as is the case with almost anything related to investing), but something like a "5/25" rule might work. A "5/25" rule dictates that you rebalance a position if either of the following conditions is met: (a) the change in the allocation of the asset class is greater than an absolute 5 percent, or (b) the change in the allocation of the asset class is greater than 25 percent of its original percentage allocation. Say what? Here goes:

Scenario 1—10 Percent Original Allocation. Imagine you invest 10 percent of your portfolio in large value domestic stock. The 5 percent rule dictates that if your allocation of large value domestic stock drifts up to 15 percent of your portfolio or down to 5 percent of your portfolio, it's time to rebalance. The 25 percent rule requires a simple calculation. Quick, what is 25 percent of 10 percent? That's right—2.5 percent. So in this case you would rebalance if the allocation of large value domestic stock drifts above 12.5 percent or below 7.5 percent. Said differently, the 25 percent rule is the governing factor, simply because it creates a lower threshold for rebalancing.

Scenario 2—30 Percent Original Allocation. Imagine you hold 30 percent of your portfolio in treasury bonds. The 5 percent rule dictates that if your allocation of treasury bonds drifts past 35 percent of your portfolio or below 25 percent of your portfolio, it's time to rebalance. Now on to the required 25-percent rule calculation. 25 percent of 30 percent is 7.5 percent. In this case we can ignore the result of the 25-percent rule calculation because it creates a higher threshold for rebalancing than the 5 percent rule. Said differently, the 5 percent rule is the governing factor, and you would rebalance when the allocation of treasury bonds in your portfolio drifts above 35 percent or below 25 percent.

Now, as a reward for suffering through some math, I'll give you the Cliffs Notes version of this rule. As it turns out, you would apply the 5-percent rule if your original allocation of the particular asset class is greater than 20 percent, and you would apply the 25-percent rule if your original asset allocation is less than 20 percent. Enough about rebalancing.

Dollar Cost Averaging

Before we move on to other topics, I should quickly walk you through the frequently bandied-about term *Dollar Cost Averaging* (DCA). The basic idea behind DCA is that an investor can reduce market risk by investing incrementally over time instead of dropping a sizable lump sum into the market. In other words, if you were contemplating investing a huge amount of money into the market (say, a large cash bonus or an inheritance) just as the market was about to go into a tailspin, you would be better off with incremental investments over time, as you would have avoided a significant loss. Sound appealing?

There is only one small problem with this theory. You know what is coming next. Imagine the voice of a cranky old professor emanating from this book. *It doesn't work.* If healthy market returns are the goal, DCA falls flat as a strategy. It's not hard to understand why. Financial markets rise more often than they fall—e.g., the S&P500 has produced an average annual return of roughly 10 percent since markets opened in 1926. As a general rule, then, the longer your funds are invested, the better you should do. Said differently, you are incentivized to invest today instead of tomorrow.

But what if you just *know* that a market correction is coming? I'll explore this fallacy in more detail later in the chapter. The truth is, we don't ever know. Remember, investing is about probability, and you are *more likely than not* to do better by investing a lump sum all at once instead of employing DCA. If DCA just feels better than jumping into the market headfirst, no sweat. Employ DCA if it helps you sleep at night. Not everyone is equipped to jump off the high dive at the neighborhood pool. If you are a nervous Nellie, the fact that you are likely to do better by investing a lump sum all at once isn't worth the anxiety that comes with this decision.

Now that we've quickly explored the concept of dollar cost averaging, we'll move to another key decision you will need to make about your investment strategy—i.e., whether to employ an active strategy, a passive management strategy, or a mixture of both.

Active v. Passive Management

You've probably noticed that I like to use the term "magical thinking." Magical thinking sits in stark opposition to reality. It's the suspension of disbelief despite objective evidence that points to a contrary conclusion, and the term applies to a healthy slice of the active management world.

Passive investment managers believe that markets are largely efficient and acknowledge that beating the market is exceptionally difficult. Instead of focusing on trying to outmaneuver other investors and therefore achieve better-than-market returns, passive investment managers try to deliver the performance of a segment of the market (or asset class) as a whole by investing very broadly in most or all of the securities in a segment or asset class.

In stark opposition to this approach, active investment managers believe that markets are inefficient. Therefore, they believe they can exploit these market inefficiencies by either (a) carefully selecting stocks that are priced incorrectly, or (b) purchasing or selling stocks at just the right time.

Here's an example of an active management strategy. Susan, an active fund manager, believes that shares of Goober, Inc. are undervalued. Further, Susan believes that the market will eventually recognize this and the share price of Goober, Inc. will rise substantially, affording her a healthy profit. By purchasing shares of Goober, Inc., Susan hopes to capitalize on the gap between what she believes to be true and the information already assimilated by the market (i.e., she inherently believes she knows something that other investors don't). This is the art of stock selection.

Another example: Susan studies sixteen different peer-reviewed papers by the world's leading economists and fervently believes that the technology sector is about to suffer devastating losses. Accordingly, she sells every technology stock inside the fund she manages. She believes that other investors haven't adequately assimilated the information in these peer-reviewed papers, and accordingly, she thinks she can "get out ahead" of the market. By selling her technology stocks, she is engaging in the art of market timing.

The ability to select winning stocks and time the market has been the hallmark of the value proposition pitched by brokers and fund managers for decades. To once again borrow the words of my cantankerous old professor, "There is only one small problem with this approach. *It generally doesn't work*." As time marches on, more and more evidence has materialized which highlights the fact that active investment management is typically a losing strategy. To make matters worse, investors pay their advisors considerable sums to produce sub-par results. What gives?

To understand how silly this is, let's return to the same concept that springs up continually when we discuss investing—probability. To graph the likelihood that any particular outcome is achieved, we can create a probability curve. In many disciplines and/or facets of life, including investing, a probability curve is often bell-shaped. This is due to the application of that other concept you now understand—standard deviation.

The following graph will tell you the probability of any particular outcome (measured by the number of times you flip heads in this case) when you flip a coin sixteen times in a row.

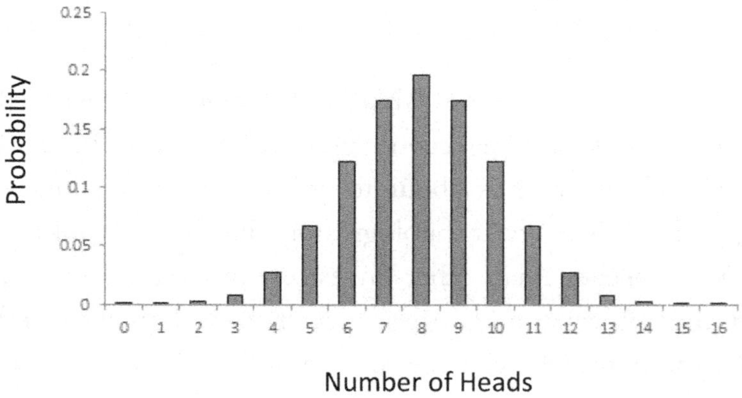

The likelihood that you flip heads sixteen times in a row is incredibly low (less than .002 percent). Conversely, the likelihood that you flip heads exactly ten times out of sixteen is much higher (12.2 percent). This coin flip example is an illustration of the principle of random chance at work.

Let's imagine that flipping heads was indeed the desired outcome. Now, riddle me this: If you could pay someone a substantial fee to shift this probability curve in the negative direction (i.e., your odds of flipping heads ten out of sixteen times will decrease from 12.2 percent to 8 percent), would you do it?

If you answered no, we're off to a good start. I'm telling you that active management doesn't usually work well, and that the odds of an active manager beating a reasonable benchmark are worse than random chance. But don't take my word for it. A veritable brain trust of experts has studied this phenomenon. In his 1998 book, *Winning the Loser's Game*, Charles Ellis arrived at the conclusion that only 20 percent of active managers outperformed appropriate risk-adjusted benchmarks.

In their 2015 book, *The Incredible Shrinking Alpha*, Larry Swedroe and Andrew Berkin explain why they believe that the track record of active managers has declined from bad to worse. Here are four of the factors they cite: (a) markets are growing increasingly efficient over time, (b) there are fewer victims for active managers to exploit, (c) the competition among active managers continually grows fiercer as better analytical tools and faster access to information becomes available, and (d) the number of funds chasing outperformance has grown exponentially. In short, the outlook for active managers has spiraled downward over the course of several decades.

The Buffet Bet. Nearly everyone has heard of Warren Buffet, one of the wealthiest men in the world and certainly one of the most acclaimed investors of all time. In 2006, he challenged the hedge fund industry, stating that over a period of ten years, an S&P 500 index fund would outperform a collection of hedge funds net of fees and that he was willing to bet $500,000 on it. An index fund simply tracks the performance of a slice of the stock market (in this case large-cap U.S. stocks) and usually charges only a small annual fee. Conversely, a hedge fund is the epitome of the active management approach. Many hedge fund managers do all sorts of fancy things (such as use derivates or leverage) in an attempt to beat the market. Hedge funds charge sizeable fees for their work; the standard is "2 and 20", meaning a 2 percent management fee and 20 percent performance fee (i.e., they take a 20 percent slice of the profit).

In late 2007, Ted Seides of Protégé Partners accepted Buffet's bet. He created a diversified basket of hedge funds and was confident he could outperform the S&P500 index fund. The ten-year period ran from January 1, 2008 to December 31, 2017. The results? Buffet and his simple index fund didn't just beat Seides. It was a bloodbath. Only months into the ten-year period, the S&P500 took its biggest loss since the Great Depression. Because hedge funds can use strategies to "hedge" against market declines (by "shorting" certain stocks, for example), Seides came out of 2008 ahead of Buffet. By the end of 2017, however, the index fund had returned 128.5 percent return net of fees and expenses, and the basket of hedge funds had returned only 36.3 percent net of fees and expenses. Notably, 60 percent of all gains achieved by the hedge fund ultimately went to pay the high fees charged by management.

Okay, you get the picture, and I imagine that you are wondering, "Why in the world would anyone drop their hard-earned dollars into a risky investment like a hedge fund?" After all, devoting capital to a passive strategy is a much safer way to accumulate wealth. When viewed in the context of the entire universe of active v. passive investments, a very clear choice seems to emerge. Indeed, logic would dictate that passive management is the only rational option, right? While this is a sensible response to what I have cited thus far, the reality is a bit more nuanced.

First, let me start with a proposition that efficient market devotees may not appreciate. Here it goes:

A select few active asset managers are extremely good at what they do.

Wait, what? Yes… I know. You might ask, "Isn't this just the 'bell curve phenomenon' at work? Doesn't probability simply indicate that while most active managers will fail at their mandate, some will succeed? In other words, should we gamble that the active manager we pick will land at the positive extreme of the bell curve? How is this better than random chance?"

Before I tackle these questions, allow me to combine my previous statement with one my efficient market colleagues *will* appreciate:

Most active asset managers are ineffective.

A colleague of mine who very successfully manages an active "deep-value" fund agrees whole-heartedly with this statement. After years at Goldman Sachs and other investment banks, he set out on his own. He found that freeing himself from the bureaucratic shackles that hampered his decision-making allowed him to capitalize on something he is very good at doing—combining rigorous financial analysis and an appetite for risk with the ability to implement or revise a strategy exceptionally quickly. My friend rolls his eyes at the hedge fund industry. He personally doesn't believe a typical hedge fund manager has the skillset to actually succeed at what he so charismatically tells clients he will do. *Smoke and mirrors*, he says.

There are a few managers, like my colleague, who really are exceptionally good at implementing a market-beating strategy. I would posit that this success is not just the result of dumb luck, but rather the combination of chance (which is always present when investing in capital markets) and a very impressive skillset. So how do active managers who beat the market for an extended period of time achieve this magical-seeming outcome? There are any number of approaches they can use, from highly quantitative approaches (i.e., using complex algorithms and the input of hundreds of PhDs in various disciplines, ala Renaissance Technologies' mind-blowingly successful Medallion Fund) to more conventional bargain-hunting techniques (i.e., "deep-value" funds and Warren Buffet's famed value-centered approach).

A quick sidebar on Renaissance Technologies' Medallion Fund: The Medallion Fund, launched by Jim Simmons, is the most successful hedge fund of all time. The fund's track record is so astounding, I question whether its performance will ever be surpassed. Medallion has returned more than 66 percent (39 percent net of fees) annually from 1988 to 2019. For perspective, this means that $1 invested in Medallion in 1988 would be worth more than $20,000 (after fees) today. This same $1 invested in a no-cost S&P500 index fund would be worth $20. A $1 investment in legendary investor Warren Buffet's Berkshire Hathaway would be worth $100.

Sounds enticing, doesn't it? I'm sorry to report that the big names who have done exceptionally well are closed to new capital. Indeed, the legendary Medallion fund bought out of all its non-employee investors long ago. This begs the key issue of how you are supposed to pick the winning asset manager of the next decade. Of course, there isn't an easy answer. Investing in last year's top-performing fund is generally a poor strategy. Investing in a fund that has a track record of achieving market-beating returns over the course of the last eight years, on the other hand, may be worth exploring, provided the fund isn't already closed to new investors.

I should note that the Securities and Exchange Commission effectively limits the opportunity to invest in hedge funds and other non-publicly traded funds (such as private equity funds and venture funds) to either "accredited investors" or "qualified clients," depending on the types of fees the fund charges. While the definition of an accredited investor became more nuanced in 2020, the basic idea is that an "accredited investor" must have at least $1 million in assets (other than equity in a primary residence) or an annual income over $200,000 ($300,000 for joint filers) going back at least two years, with a reasonable expectation that this income level will continue. To be considered a qualified client, on the other hand, an investor must either have (a) at least $1 million in assets under management with the fund immediately after entering into an investment advisory contract with the fund, or (b) a net worth of more than $2.1 million immediately before entering into an advisory contract, excluding the value of a primary residence.

Because nearly all hedge funds charge a performance fee and therefore may only take on qualified clients, you will find that many hedge funds require a minimum investment of $1 million. If a particular fund doesn't insist on a $1 million minimum investment, you may find that you need to demonstrate that you meet the $2.1 million net worth threshold required by the qualified client rule.

While drooling over storied successes like Renaissance Capital's Medallion fund is entertaining, I should redirect your attention to the reality of the industry. Most hedge funds suck, and the juicy fees these poorly performing managers charge aren't justifiable in any way. The moral of the story is clear enough. Unless you place a big premium on the excitement that comes with trying to second-guess the market, I would suggest you consider a predominantly passive approach.

To be clear, there will always be active managers who beat the market. Sadly, random chance indicates that there should be many more of them. (Remember that bell curve?) If you are lucky enough to (a) satisfy the criteria to be considered a "qualified client," and (b) meet a fund manager whose track record and approach convince you he can regularly produce outsized returns, I very strongly suggest that you limit your interest in this manager's fund to no more than 25 percent of your portfolio.

In ideal circumstances, a modest interest in a well-managed deep-value fund—a particular type of fund that produces returns that aren't strongly correlated to equity indices such as the S&P500—may nicely complement the less volatile and tried-and-true passive strategies explored below. When investors flee the market and a passive strategy responds in kind, those bargain-hunting deep-value fund managers start to salivate. Just be careful. Please make sure you understand the fees you are being charged and the true track record and strategy employed by the fund manager.

Choosing Between Two Compelling Passive Investment Strategies

Perhaps you're now convinced that most of your portfolio should be committed to a passive investment strategy. Perfect. Step one completed. Now let's examine two effective passive investment strategies: (1) indexing, and (2) structured asset class investing.

Indexing: This is the best known of all passive investment strategies. Pioneered by Vanguard (a top-notch organization founded by the venerable late Jack Bogle), indexing simply involves holding all of the stocks in a benchmark index inside a fund in exactly the same proportion as they are held in the index itself. The S&P500 index is the most commonly known index fund, but there are many others (the Russell2000 index or Vanguard total stock market index, for example). Indexing isn't limited to stock, either. Bond index funds exist as well.

If an investor carefully combines various index funds in a portfolio to ensure sufficient diversification, indexing can result in a very good investment experience. Compared to active management, indexing has the following advantages, among others:

- *Total transparency.* You will never wonder what is going on inside an index fund. The fund has a very clear charter (i.e., mission statement), and the process of adjusting the assets held in the index fund is automated.

- *No style drift.* "Style drift" is the term used to describe the migration of some of the fund's holdings across different types of assets. This is potentially a big issue with actively traded funds. You thought you were purchasing shares of a fund that solely focused on small biotech stocks, but the fund manager decided to park 20 percent of the fund in defense contractor stocks. In short, style drift makes it hard to control the composition of a portfolio.

- *Low expense ratio.* Index funds are largely automated, and it's hard to justify big management fees when a machine is doing the analytical work. A stock index fund may have an expense ratio as low as… zero. *Wait, what?* Yes, as of the writing of this book, Fidelity offers a no-cost total stock market index fund. This is called a loss leader, meaning the fund naturally operates at a loss for Fidelity and is intended to bring in new clients who will invest in other products that Fidelity offers (and which will presumably make Fidelity money).

- *Low cash drag.* Cash drag is a term used to describe a reduction in the performance of a fund because some of the fund's investable assets remain in cash. Presumably, you only purchase shares of a stock fund or bond fund because you wish to own stocks or bonds. You don't aim to "invest" in cash. If the fund manager holds significant cash inside the fund, performance is hindered. Cash drag is minimized inside index funds.

When clients ask me about indexing and want to know whether they can do better, my answer is, *Probably, but it is a bit com-pli-cated*! I'll say it again, just to make sure that we're on the same page. *Indexing is a perfectly fine strategy.* It does, however, have weaknesses.

What is coming next is one reason I suggest you tolerate the trendy phrase "The science of investing." As the son of a nuclear physicist and the grandson of a medical school professor, I have to admit I do wince a little when I hear this term. Investing doesn't initially *seem* science-y. There are those, however, who approach investing from a very rigorous, analytical, and data-driven vantage point. I say we let them wear their scientist badges with pride. You can let me know if you agree after we suffer through this next section.

Here is a brief description of a few of the weaknesses of indexing, along with a high-level overview of the concepts involved:

- *Higher Trading Costs.* Few non-advisors know that the owner (publisher) of an index (which is simply a list of stocks) releases their decision about which stocks should be included in the index once per year. This is called reconstitution. The date of reconstitution is known by traders well in advance.

Here is how Russell FTSE, which owns (publishes) a series of indexes that track distinct segments of the stock market, manages the selection of stocks for their indexes:

"On rank day in May (this year May 10), all eligible US securities are ranked by their total market capitalization. Companies whose stocks are listed on eligible stock exchanges and who pass investability rules are considered for inclusion in the indexes. Beginning on June 7, preliminary lists of additions and deletions to the indexes are communicated to the marketplace. These changes go into effect after the close on Friday, June 28."[iv]

Here's the problem: Stocks that have been dropped from an index face incredible selling pressure as index funds scramble to ditch the dropped stocks, while stocks that have been added to an index face a surge in demand as index funds scramble to buy the added stocks. This is hugely inefficient, and it is known as the reconstitution effect. It creates very high trading costs for index funds. While index funds can be excellent investments, their mandate is to reduce tracking error, not trade efficiently.

- *Migration of Assets Over Time.* You now understand that index funds reconstitute annually. This has another less-than-ideal consequence. If you prefer a data-driven, science-y approach to investing (which you should), you will carefully control your exposure to various factors of return (such as size and growth v. value—more on this later). With indexing, the capitalization of individual stocks will grow or retract over the course of a year, and as a result, the index may wind up holding stocks that no longer represent the target asset class for many months before reconstitution occurs.

- *Inclusion of All Stocks in an Index.* But wait a second, you say, isn't taking the human fallibility factor out of the equation the whole point of indexing and passive investing in general? Shouldn't it therefore be ideal to include every single stock inside an index? Good question. As compared to an index fund (the management of which is incredibly rigid), funds that target specific asset classes inside a structured portfolio have a bit of wiggle room to screen out specific types of stocks in a very disciplined way based on extensive research. Examples of stocks that more-often-than-not hinder performance of an index fund (because they have historically poor returns) include stocks in bankruptcy, "penny" (aka super cheap) stocks, stocks that have just gone through an initial public offering, and small growth stocks with low profitability despite the receipt of large investments. Index funds, because of their very clear charter to track an index with minimum tracking error, are forced to accept the inclusion of these stinker stocks in their funds.

- *Restricted Ability to Employ Tax-Savings Strategies.* Let's revisit a basic concept from the tax primer you suffered through in Chapter 2. Tax on short-term capital gains = bad. Tax on long-term capital gains = better. No tax = best. Because of their charter, index funds are not able to intentionally minimize taxes through actions such as offsetting capital gains with capital losses (although this may happen naturally to some extent) or avoiding taking any short-term gains.

- *Inability to Use Screens for Known Factors of Return.* This one is a mouthful. If it sounds like a bunch of gobbledygook, that just means that you're human (like most of us). We already discussed why including all stocks in a particular index isn't

> necessarily a good thing. Said differently, excluding a small number of stinker stocks from a large pool of stocks can enhance the overall return of a fund. To further this concept, some asset class funds held in structured portfolios will employ screens for factors such as momentum or profitability.

Momentum is a well-known (but poorly understood) phenomenon that dictates that if a stock price declines or rises over a 3-12 month period, it is likely to continue to decline or rise over the next 3-12 month period. Is it a foolproof concept? Of course not. *Good Lord*, you think. Aren't we talking about active management again? Kinda sorta, but not in the conventional manic sense of exercising unfettered discretion. A momentum screen simply means that a fund manager fund has the ability to defer on buying a stock that exhibits negative momentum—but would otherwise fall into the fund's "buy" category—until the negative momentum ceases. With positive momentum, the fund manager might hold a stock that falls into the fund's "sell" category until the positive momentum plays itself out. An index fund can't do this.

If you are still with me, I am overjoyed. The previous section approached the goobery side of the investment nerd spectrum, and if what I wrote made at least a little sense to you, believe me, you are eons ahead of most folks. Let's keep the momentum going. Next up: structured asset class investing.

Structured Asset Class Investing. Humor me by digesting another simple-minded analogy. Let's imagine your investment portfolio is a vegetable garden; the various plants you purchase represent your capital investment, and the vegetables produced by these plants represent your return. Now imagine we have three gardeners (let's call them Indexer, Average Active Trader, and Asset Class Investor) with three identical plots of land.

Indexer finds suitable places for all of his plants, ensures they get sunshine and water, and then lets the garden run wild for a year. After a year has passed, Indexer shows up and does some basic pruning to ensure that the various plants don't compete unnecessarily with each other for sunshine and nutrients.

Average Active Trader finds suitable places for all of his plants but then changes his mind repeatedly about their location, resulting in a relentless cycle of digging up and replanting. *Maybe the broccoli needs more sunshine*, he thinks, *and maybe the carrots will actually do better next to the radishes.* Average Active Trader works exceptionally hard, but he uproots his plants frequently in an attempt to get them in that ever-elusive perfect configuration.

Asset Class Investor finds suitable places for all of her plants and ensures they get plenty of sunshine and water, but unlike Indexer, she regularly weeds the garden, watches for pests, and prunes (very modestly and carefully) to ensure the plants don't complete unnecessarily with each other for sunshine and nutrients.

Now, whose garden do you suppose produces the most vegetables? Not Average Active Trader's garden. By digging up and replanting continually, Average Active Trader has created too much churn, and his plants don't have a chance to take root. At the end of several years, his garden is full of stunted plants, none of which produce many vegetables. What about Indexer? Indexer's garden produces a nice crop of vegetables, but it looks a bit wild unless you happen to visit shortly after the annual clean-up. And Asset Class Investor? Her garden is tidy, pest-free, and produces a bumper crop.

The moral of this story? Asset class investing isn't purely passive, but it sure isn't active in the traditional sense, and most importantly, it has produced attractive returns for investors for many years. The author of a 2013 Wall Street Journal article refers to Dimensional Fund Advisors (the first group of funds to champion the asset class investment strategy) as "the active-passive powerhouse." It's an interesting description, and I think it works.

Okay, enough fluff. You made it through the last section, after all, so I know you can buckle down and get through the rest of this analysis. Let's take a closer look at exactly what I mean when I use the term "structured asset class investing." I acknowledge that this descriptor runs the risk of being so vague as to be meaningless, but together we'll make sense of it. Here's my attempt at a definition:

> *Structured asset class investing is the discipline of carefully controlling exposure to various asset classes by investing in and rebalancing funds inside a portfolio that may tilt toward certain risk factors and/or employ various screens in the pursuit of diminished volatility and/or superior returns.*

The lawyer in me just winced. My definition is both wordy and imprecise—a sad combination. Regardless, let's unpack what I just wrote.

First, let's analyze what "carefully controlling exposure to various asset classes" really means. Whether an investment manager (a) purchases a series of funds that target narrow classes of assets and assembles them into an ideal portfolio or (b) purchases one or more "multi-factor" funds—i.e., a fund that targets multiple asset classes—she is tightly controlling her client's exposure to various segments of the mark.

Next, let's unravel the phrase "investing in and rebalancing funds inside a portfolio that may tilt toward certain risk factors and/or employ various screens." You already know what "investing" means, and we walked through the concept of "rebalancing."

What about "tilt toward certain risk factors?" This is a bit confusing at first, but you'll get there, I promise.

Before we discuss tilt, let's review risk factors. Remember when we walked through the various risk factors that drive returns in the stock market? The two big ones are company size and growth v. value. Small-company stocks generally have a higher standard deviation (i.e., greater volatility) and a higher average annual return than large company stocks. Value stocks (i.e., ugly mugs) generally have a higher standard deviation and a higher average annual return than growth stocks (i.e., sexy stocks).

If two stocks produced exactly the same return but had different standard deviations, you would always pick the stock with the lower standard deviation. However, in the case of value stocks and small company stocks, the increased return of these two broad asset classes over a long time horizon has historically outweighed the increased standard deviation.

Now, what does it mean to tilt a fund or portfolio? As it sounds, it simply means shifting the allocation of assets within a fund or portfolio toward a particular asset class. This can be done at the fund level (i.e., a fund manager can allocate more of the fund's assets to either value stocks or small-company stocks) or at the portfolio level (i.e., an advisor can simply allocate more of a portfolio to funds that invest solely in value stocks or small-company stocks). Either way, tilting toward value stocks and small-company stocks has proven an effective method of producing strong returns over a long time horizon.

Now, what do I mean when I write "employ various screens?" Earlier we covered the concept of momentum and explored how a fund can choose to allow the positive or negative momentum of a stock to play out before selling or buying. This is one example of a screen. Another screen that a fund might employ is related to profitability. By overweighting positions in companies that have attractive earnings-to-book value or earnings-to-assets ratios, a fund may further enhance its overall return. While the terms "earnings" and "assets" are easy to decipher intuitively, the term "book value" essentially means the value of the company according to its financial statements (roughly assets minus liabilities).

If you're still reading this, nice work. You now have at least a basic understanding of the differences between active management, indexing, and structured asset class investing. Next, let's turn to a critical decision you will need to make—i.e., whether to go it yourself or hire an investment advisor.

Self-Help v. Hiring an Advisor

As a wealth manager, I do spend a fair amount of time thinking about the value proposition that comes with hiring a professional to manage an investment portfolio. In short, in my view (which is only one of many) it comes down to the following factors, each of which we will explore in detail:

(1) *The Suck Factor.* The average human absolutely sucks at investing. A good investment advisor does not.

(2) *The Planning Factor.* An investment advisor can help integrate a carefully crafted investment strategy into a thoughtful financial plan.

(3) *The Tax Factor.* An investment advisor can help maximize the tax efficiency of a portfolio.

(4) *The Sleep-at-Night Factor.* An investment advisor can help monitor the performance of a portfolio, rebalance the assets within a portfolio, and suggest changes to the composition of the portfolio based on various life events.

The Suck Factor. Remember back when *American Idol* was the most popular show around? In case you missed this, contestants on American Idol would attempt to wow the judges with their vocal skills in an endless series of televised auditions. One of the most popular elements of the show catered shamelessly to the human predilection toward schadenfreude, which is a fancy term for a complex emotion involving the perverse sense of joy that stems from watching others fail. It is the opposite of empathy. On American Idol, this manifested itself in the early auditions, in which some contestants sang so incredibly poorly that it beggared disbelief. Off-key, warbly, and typically displaying a bizarre degree of confidence, these performers inspired a heightened sense of schadenfreude in some viewers. For others (like me) it was just sad and hard to watch.

Anyway, now you know how advisors feel when watching the average investor make mistake after mistake. The average investor is the awkward teenager in a homespun dress belting out *The Rose* in the wrong key. In a word, the average investor sucks. It's a harsh truth, and only a select few dodge this unfortunate reality. Remember the section of this book devoted to active management? Most of the Harvard PhDs and brilliant computer programmers who populate hedge funds can't get it right. Perhaps it's not surprising, then, that the average investor is even worse at actively managing a portfolio. What's less intuitive but even more important is that few investors have the discipline and foresight to stick with a sensible passive investment strategy either.

DALBAR is an organization that regularly monitors how well investors perform in comparison to the market as a whole. Each year a new report is issued, and each year it produces a bit of schadenfreude in advisors along with some head-scratching. Consider these depressing statistics: In the ten-year period from January 1, 2007 to December 31, 2017, the S&P500 returned 8.5

percent, yet the average stock investor achieved a return of only 4.88 percent. And while inflation during this period averaged 1.64 percent, the average bond investor achieved a return of only 0.48 percent. Here it is in table format for those of you who prefer visuals:

Period from December 1, 2007 to December 31, 2017

S&P 500 Index Return	8.5%
Average Stock Investor Return	4.88%
Annual Inflation	1.64%
Average Bond Investor Return	0.48%

And it's not getting better. As more and more reasonably priced investment funds that broadly track the stock market are launched, one would think that investors would get better at the "buy and hold" concept. Apparently not. In 2018, DALBAR calculated that while the S&P500 declined by 4.38 percent in 2018, the average stock investor lost 9.42 percent.

How on earth can this be? While there are a number of potential explanations, the primary force behind this awful underperformance (i.e., the suck factor) is human frailty. We are the victims of our genetic programming, and while the "fight or flight" instinct may have served us well when we were hunting wooly mammoths with spears, it has a crippling effect on our ability to remain disciplined as investors.

A good investment advisor does a fair amount of what a psychologist would call "behavioral coaching." This is the process of holding a client's hand (usually figuratively, sometimes literally) when the stock market roller coaster is just a bit too nauseating. A winning strategy: breathe, relax, go over the fundamentals again, and do nothing other than rebalance a portfolio. In summary, a good investment advisor will help you fight your own worst instincts.

One noteworthy organization I mentioned earlier, Dimensional Funds Advisors (DFA), presents an interesting case study on the impact of advisors on investor behavior. Unusual among mutual fund managers of their size ($609 billion under management as of the end of 2019), DFA requires that any individual investor who holds its funds work through an independent investment advisor who has been vetted by the organization. DFA isn't looking for investment managers who can best *sell* product. Instead, DFA is looking for advisors who understand the folly of human nature and will buckle down and remember all of the fundamentals we've discussed when the going gets rough. Evidence of the success of this approach? In 2008, the year in which the financial markets took their worst drubbing since the Great Depression, billions flowed out of mutual funds. Simultaneously, DFA advisors directed billions of new capital into DFA funds. The result? The market bounced violently off the bottom, and DFA, its advisors, and their clients, all did exceptionally well.

As I finish writing this book, financial markets are surprisingly healthy given the significant impact the Coronavirus pandemic has had on the global economy. I watched with interest as some well-known financial advisors encouraged their clients to liquidate their equity investments and hold huge cash positions. Not surprisingly, this occurred as the pandemic took hold and markets started to tremble. Some of these advisors liquidated their clients' equity positions about halfway down the market slide in March 2020. At first, the advisors celebrated their wisdom when the market bottomed out on March 20, 2020. But then these advisors (and their clients) suffered a very common fate. The market rebounded (violently), and in August of 2020, when markets bounced back, these advisors were left scratching their heads and wondering when to re-enter. In short, they locked in significant losses for their clients by exiting the market and missing the ride back up.

The Planning Factor. If the suck factor isn't compelling enough, it is worth thinking through the considerable benefit of working with a professional to not only create a retirement plan, but also to ensure that your investment strategy fits seamlessly within that plan. If you muddle your way through this book and absorb 50 percent of what I've told you, you *are* capable of constructing an adequate investment strategy and retirement plan. But should you?

Forgetting an advisor's access to effective retirement modeling software, and forgetting the resources an advisor has at her fingertips through any number of financial planning organizations and continued education, I believe an advisor is a valuable sounding board. In the United States we describe an individual's attorney as her "counsel." As someone who has both practiced as an attorney for many years and worked as a wealth manager, I can state with certainty that the term "counsel" is equally applicable to competent financial planners and investment advisors (both of whom I generally refer to as "advisors" in this book).

A good advisor will challenge your assumptions about retirement and double-check your budget, instantly evaluating it in the context of what she's learned by working with clients in similar situations. She will suggest areas of improvement, and she will help you accurately model your cash flow in retirement. She will help you craft a plan that isn't a boilerplate (off-the-shelf) solution, but a customized long-term strategy that takes your particular needs and wants into consideration.

The Tax Factor. A good advisor, often in consultation with your accountant, can help you minimize the tax implications of your investment strategy. How do they do this? Good question. That topic is addressed in Chapter 4.

The Sleep-at-Night Factor. When you envision how you will spend your time in retirement, does this include continually monitoring and maintaining your investment portfolio? If so, and you really do enjoy this stuff, you can strike this particular value proposition from the list. Don't let an advisor deprive you of this source of joy in your life.

I once had an initial consultation with an investment hobbyist who enjoyed manually inputting the share prices for his more than 100 individual stock holdings into a customized Excel spreadsheet on a daily basis. He recognized that he could get this same data with minimal effort by simply trusting the continually updated information provided by his custodian (Fidelity in this case), but he *just wanted to be sure.* After nearly blowing a mouthful of sparkling water back through my nose, I quickly (privately and without any training, of course) diagnosed this gentleman with a personality disorder. He wanted to know if I would take over the maintenance of his special spreadsheet. He didn't become a client!

To help you determine whether retirement is the right choice for you and plan for an enjoyable experience when that day arrives, in Chapter 1 I asked you to think carefully about what brings you joy. Joy is not the same thing as the absence of worry. Nevertheless, experiencing joy will be difficult (if not impossible) if your monkey mind is continually fretting about your ever-fluctuating investment portfolio. If you are like many, knowing that an advisor has one eye on the market and the other on your portfolio may provide a degree of reassurance. This is furthered by the knowledge that you will have a trusted resource at your disposal if you experience a significant change in life circumstances. It's hard to put a price-tag on sleeping soundly at night.

I noted earlier that Vanguard is the organization that pioneered the whole concept of indexing. In short, Vanguard made it exponentially easier for self-help advocates to create a reasonably balanced portfolio on their own. If anyone would champion the do-it-yourself option, you might think it would be Vanguard. But this is not the case at all. Folks at Vanguard are data-driven (bless their souls) and not prone to magical thinking. In a very interesting paper, researchers at Vanguard determined that enlisting the help of an advisor added an average of 3 percent (this is "Alpha" in investor geek parlance) to the return of an individual investor's portfolio.

Three percent is not chump change, so it's worth digging a bit deeper into how Vanguard came up with this. Here is a summary of the various elements that comprise the estimate of 3 percent in "advisor Alpha:"[v]

Strategy Employed by Advisor	Added Value to Clients (percentage of net returns)
Suitable asset allocation using broadly diversified funds	> 0%, but too unique to quantify
Cost-effective implementation	0.34%
Rebalancing	0.26%
Behavioral coaching	1.50%
Asset location	0 to 0.75%
Spending strategy	0 to 1.10%

Total-return versus income investing	> 0%, but too unique to quantify
Total potential value added	~3.0%

Will your advisor earn you an extra 3 percent return? Maybe, and maybe not. Vanguard naturally recognizes that "advisor Alpha" is extremely hard to measure, but they did their best with their study. Perhaps you are less swayed than most by the behavioral shortcomings that are an intrinsic part of our makeup as humans. Maybe "advisor Alpha" in your case is only 1.5 percent. Or more dire still, imagine that your advisor, despite all of her hard work, only manages to match the return you would have achieved on your own (beware of magical thinking here) on a fee-adjusted basis. We shouldn't assume this is a bad result. Ideally, your advisor has been a resource in countless other ways. After all, the value of an advisor should extend well beyond obtaining a desirable investment return.

How to Choose an Advisor

The title of this section presupposes that you have decided to hire an advisor. This may not be the case, and if not, I suggest that you skip this section for now, and come back later if you decide you could use some help. If you have decided that getting some help is a good step, how do you go about picking a good advisor? Unfortunately, while I do believe that most advisors mean well, it's entirely possible to find yourself working with someone who puts their own interests before yours.

Fiduciary Duty v. Suitability Standard

To understand how to pick a good advisor, first it's important to understand how the financial services industry works. This is harder than it should be. The difference between "fiduciary duty" and "the suitability standard" is often an unfamiliar one to those just getting started in their search for an advisor. To quickly summarize, an investment advisor is either subject to (a) *fiduciary duty*, which means that the advisor must always act in a client's best interests, or (b) the *suitability standard*, which means only that the advisor need merely select investments that are "suitable" for a client.

This difference is incredibly important. A fiduciary is not allowed to sell you a financial product that results in a huge commission when better options exist that would earn the advisor less. An advisor merely subject to the "suitability" standard may very well do exactly that.

Fee-Only v. Commission-Based

Now that you understand the important concept of fiduciary duty, I want you to consider the importance of working with a fee-only, independent financial advisor. Though it sounds intuitive, I have found that clients are often confused by the phrase "fee-only." Fee-only does not mean that an advisor charges clients an hourly rate or uses a flat-fee structure. While there are indeed financial planners who work this way, most fee-only advisors who develop long-term relationships with their clients charge a fee based on a percentage of assets under management. In other words, fee-only simply means that instead of getting juicy commissions for selling financial products or making trades, a fee-only advisor is only paid for her advice. For example, a typical fee-only advisor managing a $500,000 portfolio may charge 1 percent of assets under management annually (i.e., $5,000 per year), and this fee will include both monitoring and rebalancing a portfolio and providing a broad array of financial planning services. What a fee-only advisor won't do is accept a commission for selling a particular investment to a client.

To understand why this matters so much, please consider the sad story of Hiromi and Gene, an elderly couple who walked into my office several years ago. A delightful pair, Hiromi and Gene are always ready with a smile or a kind word, and they are very slow to find fault with anyone. After the usual pleasantries, they presented me with their investment portfolio, and my heart sank. What I found was layer upon layer of incredibly complex life insurance policies and horribly expensive annuities. Not a single mutual fund, stock, or bond was to be found, and not because Hiromi and Gene had an aversion to financial markets. In fact, Hiromi and Gene had a relatively high appetite for risk, largely because each of them received substantial monthly payments from valuable government pensions. Indeed, they clearly cited strong portfolio growth as a primary long-term goal.

While not the victims of outright fraud, Hiromi and Gene had simply walked into the wrong advisor's office based on the advice of a friend. When pressed, it was clear that they had absolutely no idea how any of the life insurance policies or annuities worked. In short, their portfolio was a complete mess, and what I instantly knew (and they were surprised to hear) was that their advisor had garnered tens of thousands of dollars in commissions by purchasing questionable investments on their behalf. Was the advisor in this case acting in the best interests of Hiromi and Gene? Not by a long shot. But had he purchased "suitable" investments? Legally, perhaps. While he may avoid any disciplinary action due to the looseness of the "suitability" standard, his behavior would have been a severe breach of the fiduciary duty. And as you gathered, his business model was the perfect counterpoint to a "fee-only" arrangement.

Although more and more advisors are fiduciaries (a good thing, of course), there are still a huge number who are not. Let's examine this in the context of the various types of professionals you will find in the financial services industry. We'll start with the old stockbroker model (which is still around, albeit disguised with a confusing array of titles).

Stockbroker. I want to be careful not to unfairly and categorically demonize stockbrokers. A close family friend spent his entire career working as a very successful stockbroker at a well-known firm. As a stockbroker, he was ethical, thoughtful, and cared deeply about his clients. Yes, he was paid commissions for placing clients in certain products, but he demonstrated time and again that this didn't dictate his behavior. Interestingly enough, he began planning for retirement just as the concept of fiduciary duty was gaining traction in the financial services world (i.e., the early twenty-first Century). I strongly believe that if he were to start over today, he would be an independent financial advisor.

Stockbrokers are often compensated with commissions for selling clients certain investments and/or placing trades. This form of compensation can very clearly create a questionable set of incentives when it comes to encouraging stockbrokers to place their clients' needs ahead of their own. The important takeaway here: Stockbrokers are not fiduciaries.

Independent Registered Investment Advisor. Independent Registered Investment Advisors (RIAs) are professional independent advisory firms that provide personalized financial advice to their clients. Unlike stockbrokers, RIAs are fiduciaries, and they are not beholden to the financial interests of a particular bank, insurance company, or firm. RIAs receive compensation in the form of fees for providing financial advice and investment management, and they are required to act as a <u>fiduciary</u>—i.e., they are required to act in the best interests of their clients at all times. They are registered with either the Securities and Exchange Commission or state securities regulators.

Wealth Manager. The terms "wealth manager" and "wealth management" are as overused in the financial services world as the adjective "artisanal" is in the culinary world. Like a cheeseburger served up by your local fast-food joint tantalizingly described as an artisanal creation, many a traditional stockbroker has been rebranded a wealth manager. Because the title "wealth manager" is not regulated, understand that simply because someone calls herself a wealth manager in no way means that she is a fiduciary.

If you consider working with someone who brands herself a wealth manager, first ensure that she is an independent financial advisor and will act as a fiduciary for you. Many wealth managers are not fiduciaries. For example, you will find the title frequently used by stockbrokers at major firms and thinly disguised sales professionals at banks. Once you've clarified that your prospective wealth manager is a fiduciary—you can look up advisors on the SEC's 'advisor search' tool online and ensure that they have filed a form called an ADV Part 2A if you are in doubt—do a little prodding to ensure that she is more than an artisanal cheeseburger—i.e., make sure that she isn't using the title *wealth manager* misleadingly. To intelligently ask your prospective advisor about her chosen title, we need to unravel what the term "wealth management" should mean.

Breadth of expertise is the hallmark of wealth management. As a result, a concise definition of wealth management as a singular discipline doesn't exist. In its broadest sense, wealth management is a combination of financial and legal services intended to help clients increase, preserve, or distribute their wealth. These services include investment management, financial planning, estate planning, tax planning, and philanthropic counseling. I suggest that an individual who specializes in only one of these services is not a wealth manager, while a professional who has expertise in three or more of the following areas may indeed be a wealth manager:

- *Investment Management.* If you've made it this far, you already know quite a bit about investment management—i.e., the process of selecting investments for inclusion in a portfolio, monitoring the performance of these investments, and rebalancing the portfolio. Investment management may comprise the largest portion of a wealth manager's practice.

- *Financial Planning.* Financial planning is the process of establishing and refining a client's financial goals while monitoring progress toward measurable milestones. Financial planning can include creating a plan to help a client launch a business, purchase real estate, retire comfortably, or leave behind a thoughtful legacy. Retirement planning, the primary focus of this book, is a subset of financial planning.

- *Estate Planning.* Estate planning involves drafting various legal documents to ensure the orderly management and/or disposition of a client's assets (i.e., his or her estate) in the event of disability or death. While many financial advisors are familiar with the basics of estate planning, only an attorney is permitted to offer legal advice regarding planning techniques and draft the required paperwork.

- *Tax Planning.* While preparing and submitting tax returns is the domain of certified public accountants and registered tax preparers, a good wealth manager will have a deep knowledge of important tax principles that materially impact a client's investment strategy. Tax planning can be as straightforward as analyzing whether investing in a pre-tax

401(k) or a Roth 401(k) is preferable, or as complex as analyzing how to best shield a very large estate from estate tax.

- *Philanthropic Counseling.* A wealth advisor who is well-versed in philanthropic counseling will help her clients come up with a gifting strategy that both (a) achieves her charitable objectives and reflects her values, and (b) also leads to a tax-efficient result.

Perhaps now you are better equipped to determine whether any one of the many different flavors of financial professionals out there is a good fit. While the importance of the fiduciary standard and the meaning of "fee-only" may be clear to you, what about the issue of education and professional designations/credentials? The education issue is difficult to parse without offending someone. That disclaimer aside, would you prefer to work with an advisor with a degree from Stanford (yay!), UCLA (yay!) or NYU (yay!) or a two-year degree from Post-Penitentiary Community College (hmmm…)? Enough said. You decide.

The financial services industry is positively overflowing with professional designations. We all know what a Certified Public Accountant (CPA) does, and the legal profession has been around for millennia. But what about a CFP, CFA, CPWA, ChFC, or CIMA? I won't even bother trying to capture every conceivable appendage to an advisor's last name, as many of them seem truly absurd.

I received an interesting lesson in the questionable value of lesser-known credentials when I took a week-long coaching class. The class was quite helpful, and I do feel that I finished the week with an enhanced ability to coach my clients on issues that arise in my line of work. In other words, the class had real value. I was somewhat alarmed, however, when I learned that this one-week class qualified me to take a certification exam. If I passed the exam (everyone does, apparently), I could hold myself out as a type of life coach, complete with fancy title and annual dues. *No thanks.*

But I digress. Here's a quick guide to a few of the more commonly known designations in the world of financial services:

- *Certified Financial Planner™ (CFP)®.* To become a CFP, a financial professional must demonstrate competency in a wide range of topics pertinent to wealth management, to include financial planning, tax planning, estate planning, and investment management.

- *Chartered Financial Analyst (CFA).* Becoming a Chartered Financial Analyst (CFA) is a very rigorous process and involves passing a challenging series of tests involving complex financial analysis. CFAs have demonstrated a deep knowledge of financial markets and investment strategy.

- *Certified Private Wealth Advisor® (CPWA).* Certified Private Wealth Management certification is a relatively new addition to the pantheon of possible credentials for wealth managers, and there appears to be significant overlap with the Certified Financial Planner designation, albeit with a focus on issues relevant to high-net-worth clients.

- *Chartered Financial Consultant® (ChFC).* Like the CFP designation, ChFC certification focuses on financial planning. The curriculum and examination cover the standard array of financial planning concerns, including insurance, taxation, retirement planning, investment management, and analysis and estate planning.

- *Certified Investment Management Analyst® (CIMA).* As the title of the credential implies, CIMA certificants often work as investment consultants or investment advisors, and the exam focuses on topics such as portfolio performance, risk assessment, and traditional and alternative investments.

While working with an advisor who holds at least one professional designation seems sensible, I also know of numerous advisors with no such qualification who are perfectly competent. Here's one way to tackle the conundrum of how to evaluate an advisor without any professional designation. If the advisor you are considering hiring meets the following criteria, she may be a perfectly fine choice: (a) she is salty—i.e, she's worked in the field for some time, (b) she has an excellent reputation in the community, (c) she is a fiduciary, (d) she can clearly articulate her preferred investment strategy, <u>and</u> (e) she can maintain eye contact without sweating or twitching excessively. If she doesn't satisfy these criteria, I would strongly suggest that you politely move along.

Considering an advisor with a professional designation does have two key advantages: (a) a professional designation demonstrates at least a basic degree of competence in the field, and (b) some professional designations (CFP, for example) require that credential-holders adhere to the fiduciary duty at all times. In summary, while not all good advisors are credentialed, if you don't otherwise have a means of screening out potential advisors, narrowing the crowded field of investment professionals by focusing on those that have a credential may be sensible.

CHAPTER 4

How, Part II

Creating Stable Retirement Income

A Bit of History

In the sepia-hued images of yesteryear that some nostalgic folks embrace, everyone had a pension, and deciphering how to manage cash flow required little thought. Between that General Motors monthly pension and that newfangled thing called Social Security, Grandpappy and Grandma sailed off into the sunset with nary a care in the world. It is easy to poke holes in this fantasy, but as a general rule, creating income in retirement cycled through a bell curve over the course of the twentieth century. In 1899, thirteen large corporations offered traditional pensions, but most folks were on their own when it came to creating income in retirement.[vi] After all, there is a reason that the agrarian model required producing children to survive. When you were too old to run the farm, your kids took over. Either that or you died with a hoe in your hand at age sixty (life expectancy in 1900 was only 49 years).[vii]

By mid-century, pensions had become de rigueur in many professions. Certainly government employees participated in pension plans (they still do), most large employers offered pensions, and union employees enjoyed pensions. By 1970, 26.3 million private-sector employees (about 45 percent of all private-sector workers) were covered by a pension plan.[viii] For many of us, this is where the sepia-hued images come from. Dad, or grandpa, or great-grandpa (for the youngsters out there) may have eased into retirement with nary a change in income, and when he passed away, his beloved wife may have continued to receive stable monthly income until her death.

In the latter years of the twentieth century, pension plans started to suffer. In a classic example of embracing present pleasure at the expense of future pain, many plans offered juicy benefits to retirees while making unrealistic assumptions about the future, and the incredible cost of providing significant monthly benefits to retirees became an untenable burden. As a result of this phenomenon, and the (somewhat obvious) realization that pensions are incredibly expensive, the private sector started to abandon the traditional pension as a retirement vehicle.

In the meantime, another type of retirement plan had been gaining traction. With the Revenue act of 1978, Congress paved the way for the *qualified defined contribution plan,* which to most of us means a 401(k) (though there are now many flavors of defined contribution plans). By 1990, the percentage of private-sector workers covered by a traditional pension had declined to 43 percent, while the number of private sector workers who only had access to a defined contribution plan rose to11.5 million. By 1999, 60.4 million private-sector workers were covered by defined contribution plans, and by 2006, only 20 percent of all private-sector workers were covered by defined benefit plans, while 43 percent of all private-sector workers were covered by defined contributions plans.[ix] You get the idea. The trend away from private-sector pensions and toward defined contribution plans continues.

The result of all of this? Most retirees must think much harder about how to generate income in retirement than they did fifty years ago. The shift away from the easy-to-understand monthly income generated by traditional pensions to the much more challenging self-generated income from defined contribution plans has had a tremendous impact on retirees.

In this chapter, we will examine how to generate steady income in retirement. I'll start by analyzing how individuals who enjoy significant income from traditional pensions can optimize their investment portfolio and enjoy healthy supplemental income, and I'll then dive into the more complicated issue of how those of us without a traditional pension (other than Social Security) can generate a steady stream of income in retirement without a significant risk of running dry in our golden years.

The Rare Guarantee—Withdrawal Timing for Those Who Enjoy a Strong Pension

While the percentage of the workforce that enjoys a traditional pension plan has shrunk considerably over the past few decades, there are still a large number of individuals who receive monthly pension payments from a source other than Social Security. Federal employees, State employees, County employees, and City employees often receive significant monthly pension payments in retirement, and certain private-sector companies (Kaiser Permanente comes to mind) still offer their employees incredibly generous traditional pensions. In the previous chapter, we explored how having access to a traditional pension plan may increase an investor's capacity for risk. In this chapter, we will explore how having a traditional pension plan may influence income generation strategies due to a generally lower need for self-generated income.

We've already analyzed the fact that trying to increase the rate of return in an investment portfolio by timing trades (or "outsmarting the market") is generally a losing proposition. However, this is different from demonstrating the ability to sit tight and limit withdrawals from investment or retirement accounts when the market has *already* started taken a beating. Note the past tense here. While assuming that we know when the market has bottomed out in any particular downtown is absurd (no one knows), negative momentum might persuade a patient retiree who has plenty of pension income to sit on her hands and leave her portfolio untouched. Remember our earlier analysis of why taking distributions from an account at market lows is particularly painful?

In short, an investor who can cover her monthly expenses with regular monthly pension payments is in an enviable position. This investor has discretion when it comes to pulling income from a taxable investment account. Here is an example of how this works. Harold is a retired military physician with an annual pension of $100,000. He served for thirty years as a Colonel in the Air Force, and he is now fifty-five years old. The post-tax value of his pension payments is approximately $80,000 per year, and his annual budget is approximately $70,000 per year.

Harold has his eye on a big purchase. He took advantage of highly subsidized flying lessons while he was serving in the military, and while he has an active pilot's license, he has never owned a plane. He wants to generate $90,000 to purchase a Cessna by selling assets inside his taxable investment account. Imagine that after a nice five-year run, the market (pick an index) has dropped significantly, and Harold's investment account has dropped from $1,000,000 to $700,000. Harold is in no hurry to purchase the plane, so he patiently waits for the market to recover before liquidating the required funds inside his account.

Remember, while market movements are often fitful when viewed over any long time horizon, the consistent trend is upward movement, and while anticipating the perfect moment to take a distribution is nearly impossible, avoiding taking a huge beating when the market drops precipitously is indeed possible for retirees who don't need funds immediately. Food for thought: From 1950 to 2018, the S&P500 materially dropped from a previous all-time high eleven times. In seven out of eleven instances, it took less than a year for the index to recover to its previous level. In the worst instance (following the dot-com bubble burst in 2000), it took the index eight years to recover to its previous level. While an investor like Harold may not be willing to wait eight years to purchase his Cessna, he likely has the fortitude to sit it out for at least a year.

Much of what I've spent the past page describing may seem obvious. Those who enjoy discretion with respect to when to withdraw from an investment account (or defer on taking distributions from a pre-tax retirement account—i.e., if they are under age 70 ½) enjoy the luxury of thinking hard about when to chip away at their nest egg. Fasten your seat belt and don't get too comfortable, though. The analysis regarding how to best generate income for those of us who have no pension other than Social Security is significantly more challenging.

Income Generation for the Rest of Us

If you don't have access to any pension scheme other than Social Security, you are in good company. As of 2018, only 13 percent of private-sector workers participate in a traditional pension plan.[x] Throw all public sector employees into the mix, and the overall percentage of workers participating in a traditional pension plan rises to 22 percent. In short, most of us rely on two sources of income in retirement: (a) Social Security payments, and (b) a self-made pension which is chiseled out of a mix of defined contribution plans and taxable investment accounts. We'll start with an analysis of the somewhat byzantine Social Security regime and then move into an exploration of intelligent strategies for managing a self-made pension.

Social Security

First, a word of caution. It would be foolish to rely on the Social Security Administration (SSA) to guide you toward the most sensible strategy regarding when you should elect to file for benefits given your individual life circumstances. The issue of when to file for benefits is surprisingly complex and depends on factors such as your earnings history, age, marital status, and disability. A huge number of resources exist that can help determine when to best file for benefits, from Social Security planning software to an advisor who specializes in the field. Nonetheless, my hope is that this chapter will provide you with an overview of the basic structure of the Social Security regime and the important factors that merit consideration when determining when to file for benefits.

The Fundamentals. Social Security is a pension scheme intended to provide retirement, survivor and disability benefits to qualified individuals. The SSA calculates your benefit based on three primary factors: (a) your year of birth, (b) the date upon which you elect to receive benefits, and (c) your lifetime earnings. If you are a typical salaried employee, both you and your employer pay into Social Security and Medicare through FICA taxes. Your portion of FICA is typically withheld from your paycheck, while your employer's portion of FICA is paid directly on your behalf. Self-employed individuals pay both the employer's and employee's share of FICA (which is generally referred to as the "self-employment tax").

To be eligible to receive Social Security payments, you generally need to have worked for ten full years (forty quarters). Your monthly benefit is calculated based on your highest thirty-five years of earnings, and a zero is plugged in for each year you didn't receive any earnings. This means that if you were a starving grad student with no income until age twenty-six, and then you elect to retire at age fifty, there will be a rather daunting eleven years of zero income plugged into the benefit equation. More on that later.

Here is a quick tutorial on the terminology used by the SSA that you need to know. Your Primary Insurance Amount (PIA) is the retirement benefit you will receive at your Full Retirement Age (FRA) based on your Average Indexed Monthly Earnings (AIME). What fun. Leave it to the government to distill this all down to a series of confusing acronyms. Here is a table of acronyms to help keep you organized.

Social Security Acronyms
PIA = Primary Insurance Amount
FRA = Full Retirement Age
AIME = Average Indexed Monthly Earnings

To calculate your monthly benefit, first the SSA calculates your AIME. While SSA does do this for you (of course), it's helpful to understand the steps involved. Here is how AIME is calculated:

1. Make a year-by-year list of your earnings, excluding any earnings for each year that exceeded the maximum amount subject to Social Security tax.

2. Adjust your earnings from prior years to today's dollars using the appropriate factor.

3. Select your thirty-five highest-earning years.

4. Calculate the sum of your earnings for those thirty-five years.

5. Divide by 420 (the number of months in thirty-five years).

Next, the SSA calculates your PIA based on your AIME. Here is how you calculate your PIA in 2019:

1. First, calculate 90 percent of any AIME up to $96.
2. Next, calculate 32 percent of any AIME between $960 and $5,785.
3. Then, calculate 15 percent of any AIME above $5,785.
4. Finally, add the three numbers together and you've calculated your PIA.

Here is how this looks in graphic format:

Figure 1. Computation of a Worker's Primary Insurance Amount (PIA) in 2020

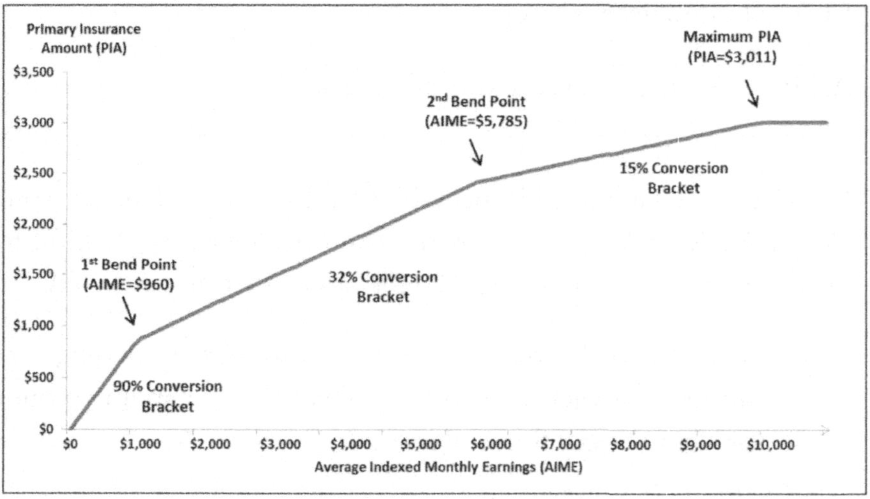

Source: Congressional Research Service (CRS).

To understand the idea behind the SSA's use of AIME as it pertains to PIA, it's helpful to convert the numbers back to annual figures. With that done, the strategy the SSA employs becomes clearer. In short, Social Security in our example replaces:

- 90 percent of the first $11,112 of average annual wage-inflation-adjusted earnings, plus

- 32 percent of average annual wage-inflation-adjusted earnings from $11,112 to $66,996, plus
- 15 percent of average annual wage-inflation-adjusted earnings from $66,996 to $123,552

Now that the concepts of AIME and PIA are at least a bit clearer, we need to explore how Full Retirement Age (FRA) impacts the analysis. First, your FRA is dependent on the year in which you were born. Here is a table that allows you to quickly determine your FRA:

Year of Birth	Full Retirement Age (FRA)
1943-1954	66
1955	66 and 2 months
1956	66 and 4 months
1957	66 and 6 months
1958	66 and 8 months
1959	66 and 10 months
1960 and later	67

Now let's look at the impact that FRA has on your PIA if you were born in 1954 or later. Here's how it works:

Age when you claim benefits	Amount of retirement benefits
4 years before FRA	75% of PIA

3 years before FRA	80% of PIA
2 years before FRA	86.67% of PIA
1 year before FRA	93.7% of PIA
at FRA	100% of PIA
1 year after FRA	108% of PIA
2 years after FRA	116% of PIA
3 years after FRA	124% of PIA
4 years after FRA	132% of PIA

Two themes become clear in this analysis: (1) the SSA incentivizes working longer and therefore disincentivizes early retirement, and (2) the SSA sensibly incentivizes individuals who are optimistic about their life expectancy to wait longer before filing for benefits. To finish our basic overview of Social Security, we need to examine the spousal benefit, ex-spouse benefit, survivor benefit, and disability benefit.

Spousal Benefit. If you are married, you don't need to have worked to collect a Social Security Benefit if (a) you have been married for at least one year, and (b) your spouse has already filed for benefits. Naturally, this benefit is particularly valuable for couples in which one spouse was a homemaker and never earned a significant income. A spouse who only earned modest income can elect to take the larger of (a) a spousal benefit (which is a maximum of one-half of the higher earner's benefit), or (b) his or her own benefit. While we will later explore how electing to defer benefits until age seventy can be a sensible strategy, this does not apply to a spousal benefit. Said differently, a spousal benefit is limited to a maximum of 50 percent of the higher earner's PIA. Below is a table that illustrates how this works for those born prior to 1955:

Filing Age	Higher Earner's Retirement Benefit as Percentage of PIA	Spousal Benefit as Percentage of Higher Earner's PIA
62	75%	35%
66	100%	50%
70	132%	50%

Here's an example of the spousal benefit in action. Fred is seventy years old and has decided to file for social security benefits. His wife, Susan, is sixty-six years old. Let's imagine that Fred has worked full-time for decades and has a PIA of $2,800. Susan, conversely, has only worked sporadically over the last few decades and accordingly has a PIA of $800. Because he is seventy, Fred's monthly benefit will be $3,696. Susan, on the other hand, can choose to either take her own benefit or 50 percent of Fred's PIA.

First, attentive reader, I have a question for you. Which is larger, 50 percent of Fred's PIA or 100 percent of Susan's own PIA? (If you get this wrong, I'm sending you back to elementary school). Clearly half of Fred's PIA ($1,400) is larger than Susan's PIA ($800). What if Susan elects to file for benefits at age seventy? Her own benefit rises (to $1,056), but is still significantly less than 50% of Fred's PIA ($1,400). Here's the kicker: Susan's spousal benefit doesn't increase at all if she waits until age seventy to take it. Put bluntly, Susan would be very foolish to wait until she is age seventy to file for benefits. Instead, she should immediately file for her spousal benefit of $1,400 per month. Together with Fred's benefit of $3,696 per month, the couple will have a respectable $5,096 in combined Social Security benefits.

I would be remiss if I didn't quickly address the old "file and suspend" trick. File and suspend was a Social Security claiming strategy that allowed married couples who had reached full retirement age to receive spousal benefits and delay retirement credits at the same time. This is how it worked: The higher-earning spouse (let's imagine it was the husband) would file for benefits at his full retirement age, and then his wife would file for spousal benefits. The husband would then immediately "suspend" his benefits and accrue additional delayed retirement credits. In the meantime, the wife would receive a spousal benefit, but she would simultaneously receive delayed retirement credits on her own account. When both spouses reached age seventy, they would each simply collect their maximum possible Social Security benefits on their own accounts, but they would have benefited from a spousal benefit for several years.

The reason I won't spend additional time explaining file and suspend is simple. The strategy was eliminated by legislation in 2016. Now "deeming" rules dictate that if one spouse qualifies for both a retirement and a spousal benefit, and she applies for one of them, she will be "deemed" to be filing for the other type of benefit as well. In other words, she can't pick which benefit she wants, and instead she will be paid whichever benefit is higher. (This defeats the purpose of file and suspend). Confusing? Absolutely. Just know that it's not terribly relevant today, but I am routinely asked about file and suspend, so I wanted you to have access to the fundamentals of the maneuver.

While file and suspend is effectively dead, if you were born in 1953 or earlier, there is still a rather obscure way to take advantage of a loophole in SSA rules that's unavailable to younger folks. It's called filing a "restricted application" and the SSA itself often struggles with this. In short, if you get on the phone with an SSA rep and they tell you that you can't do what I'm about to describe, get a supervisor on the phone. Apparently, this is a source of confusion even within the agency. So what is a "restricted application," anyway?

Ideal candidates for the "restricted application" strategy are dual-earning spouses who each have a significant Social Security account. First, imagine that spouses are fairly close in age. To file a restricted application, the older of the two—this time imagine it's the wife—submits a "restricted application" for spousal benefits based on the husband's record when the husband reaches full retirement age. At age seventy, the wife then switches to her own increased retirement benefit. Conversely, if there is a big difference in the ages of the spouses, a different variation on restricted filing can also work well. In this instance, the wife claims benefits whenever it suits the couple (perhaps at age seventy for the highest possible benefit), and the husband claims the restricted spousal benefit at age sixty-six and then switches to a higher benefit at age seventy.

The Ex-Spouse Benefit. If you were previously married for at least ten years and you haven't remarried, you may be eligible to collect Social Security based on your former spouse's PIA. Unlike the spousal benefit, to collect the ex-spouse benefit your former spouse need not have started collecting Social Security. Instead, your former spouse must simply be eligible to start collecting Social Security (i.e., he or she must have attained age sixty-two). Just like the spousal benefit, the amount collected using the ex-spouse benefit may not exceed 50 percent of your ex-spouse's PIA. In other words, if you plan on filing based on a former spouse's benefit, there is no reason to delay electing to receive Social Security beyond your own full retirement age.

A few more details about the ex-spouse benefit: As noted above, you can file for ex-spouse benefits even if your ex-spouse hasn't filed yet, but only if you were married for ten years or more. Further, if you do elect to file for ex-spouse benefits, this will have no impact on your ex-spouse's benefit. Also, you can't collect your ex-spouse benefit if you remarry. And finally, if your ex-spouse passes away, you may be entitled to survivor benefits (described in more detail below).

The Survivor Benefit. If your spouse passes away, you are eligible to receive the larger of (a) your spouse's benefit, and (b) your benefit. To qualify for this, you must have been married for more than nine months. In a deviation from the normal rules, you can take your survivor benefit at age sixty if you like. Just keep in mind that your benefit will be reduced according to the SSAs actuarial calculations for early filing (i.e., your benefit will be reduced a bit more than would be the case had you elected to take the benefit at sixty-two).

Just like both the spousal benefit and the ex-spouse benefit, there is no reason to delay taking a survivor benefit beyond your own full retirement age, as the benefit does not increase. If you have a substantial record of earnings and will be entitled to a substantial Social Security benefit based on your own record, you should consider taking your survivor benefit as soon as possible while letting your own Social Security benefits grow. This would result in ten years of benefits at a reduced rate prior to a substantial boost in Social Security benefits at age seventy.

Disability Benefit. A detailed analysis of Social Security disability benefits is beyond the scope of this book. Nevertheless, you should know that if you are forced into early retirement for health reasons prior to reaching your full retirement age, you should consider applying for Social Security disability benefits. Upon qualification, you might receive a benefit equivalent to your PIA. This could continue until you reach your full retirement age, at which point your Social Security Benefit will convert to a standard full retirement benefit (i.e., there will be no reduction based on the fact that you received disability payments prior to your standard retirement age). Further, you can choose to suspend your benefits upon reaching your full retirement age, which, in turn, leads to 8 percent growth in your benefit per year until you reach age seventy.

When Should You File? The answer to the question of when you should file for Social Security is contingent on a number of factors, and foremost among them is (a) your health and associated life expectancy, and (b) your financial need early in retirement. If you could predict your date of death with perfect accuracy, this analysis would be easy (and your life would become fodder for a Lifetime drama). Alas, it's a guessing game for most of us. Nonetheless, health and family history are two good indicators of what you might expect. If your Grandpa Nelson, Grandma Mildred, Great Uncle Butters and Great Aunt Irma all lived for a solid century, and both of your parents and Uncle Jeb are still walking twelve miles a day in their nineties, rest assured that family history is on your side. If you combine this family history with a low resting heart rate, a low-stress lifestyle, and plenty of exercise and healthy eating, you may very well live to be 105. In that event, doing anything other than deferring taking your Social Security until age seventy would be foolish. If you live roughly twenty years longer than your actuarial life expectancy, not only will you blow the SSA's calculations out of the water, but you will also likely need that larger benefit, as twenty extra years in a retirement home and/or managed care can be quite expensive.

Conversely, if you have a family history of heart disease and/or cancer and your idea of exercise consists of walking down your driveway to your mailbox once per day, taking your Social Security benefit at age sixty-two might make sense, depending on the needs of your spouse. Remember, if you pass away and you are married, your spouse gets to take the higher of your two benefits. In some instances, holding off on electing to receive Social Security until a later age (despite poor health) so that your spouse receives a substantially higher survivor benefit makes good sense.

Remember the budgeting drill back in Chapter 2? The question of whether financial need dictates that you take your benefit early is driven by your budget. In most instances, if you absolutely need the supplemental income provided by reduced Social Security payments at age sixty-two, you're in a bit of trouble, but that isn't universally true. Expecting a large inheritance in a few years, and struggling in the meantime? Taking your benefit early may be a sensible choice. Likewise, if you are helping to raise your grandchildren and accordingly you are holding off on selling your uber-valuable, paid-off primary residence for a few years, it may be wise to take your Social Security benefit early to make your budget manageable until that huge influx of cash from the sale of your home materializes.

The scenarios above notwithstanding, deferring Social Security benefits as long as possible and viewing the payments as a form of longevity insurance is my preferred approach for clients who can manage their current monthly budgets without Social Security payments. If you think of your Social Security benefit this way, you are effectively dodging the (often sky-high) premium you would have to pay to an insurance company for a private annuity, and instead you are letting the SSA handle this for you. Because your Social Security benefit increases by 8 percent for each year of deferral past your full retirement age, you are effectively trading this for the loss of one year of benefits (based on your calculated life expectancy). It's an efficient strategy, and it's actuarially sound.

The concept of Social Security "going bankrupt" gets thrown around quite a bit. This is very misleading, and while I celebrate the possibility that the fear that Social Security will simply dry up may motivate younger generations to work diligently to fully fund their 401(k)s, I don't want anyone to lose sleep unnecessarily. Social Security will not go bankrupt, or implode, or dry up, or be gobbled up by an angry space alien.

For clarity, Social Security is currently about 75 percent funded. Not ideal, but not catastrophic either. This essentially means that benefits may eventually decrease to the level that can be sustained by then-current contributions. Of course, there are many ways that Congress can correct the issue such as increasing the retirement age or increasing the Social Security tax for both employers and employees. To be sure, the longer Congress waits to address the issue, the more profound it will become. Nevertheless, if watercooler talk about Social Security evaporating in ten years has you chewing your fingernails, please take a deep breath and remember that not only is Social Security better funded than many assume, but it is also an incredibly charged issue that has a profound impact on millions upon millions of retirees. Having worked on Capitol Hill in my youth, I will tell you one thing: Old people vote, and old people ain't shy about voicing their complaints, and this makes a difference. And if I'm wrong and angry space aliens do gobble up the SSA, I will fully refund the cost of this book.

<u>The Self-Made Pension</u>

Now that you've waded through a brief exploration of Social Security, let's turn to what I hope will be a significant component of your income in retirement—the self-made pension. The self-made pension is so named because it requires you (or your advisor, if you elect to work with one) to essentially create a stream of income out of your investment portfolio. It takes a great deal more work and a great deal more discipline than collecting a monthly pension (or private annuity) check, but in the hands of a sensible investor, the strategy can work quite well.

There are three primary pillars of a self-made pension: (1) tax-deferred (or "pre-tax") defined contribution plans, (2) Roth IRAs or Roth 401(k)s, and (3) taxable investment accounts. Each has different tax attributes, and by drawing from the accounts in a sensible order, you can maximize the longevity of your portfolio. Advisors have often assumed that withdrawals should first come from taxable accounts, then from tax-deferred accounts, and finally from Roth accounts. While exceptions do exist (and we'll explore a few of them), here is the general idea:

Once you reach age 70 ½, you are subject to Required Minimum Distributions (RMDs) from your tax-deferred account. As you know by now, every distribution from a tax-deferred account is taxed at regular income tax rates. Because we have a progressive tax regime, we are incentivized not to pile up excessive income in our later retirement years and "waste" opportunities to take income and pay little tax in our early retirement years. If you'd like to dig into some meatier analysis, a very good study on the topic of tax-efficient withdrawal strategies is the appropriately titled, "Tax-Efficient Withdrawal Strategies," by Kirsten A. Cook, William Meyer, and William Reichenstein in the March/April 2015 issue of the *Financial Analysts Journal.*

As always, it's helpful to think through an example to understand how this works. Imagine that John and Suzy Dinglehopper have accumulated the following balances in their investment and retirement accounts: (a) an $800,000 investment portfolio with modest built-in capital gains, (b) two Rollover IRAs (tax-deferred) worth a combined $1,700,000, and (c) two Roth IRAs worth a combined $200,000. Let's further imagine that John and Suzy are each fifty-five years old and they are eagerly contemplating early retirement. John's projected Social Security benefit if he waits until seventy to receive benefits is $3,000 per month, and Suzy's projected Social Security benefit if she waits until seventy to receive benefits is $3,100.

Let's look at the tax implications of potential self-made pension scenarios for the Dinglehoppers. The first obvious point: John and Suzy must not lay a finger on their Rollover IRAs because they haven't yet reached age 59 ½—i.e., paying income tax and a penalty on distributions would make no sense. Second point: The capital-gains-tax-free growth of Roth IRAs is quite appealing, and holding out on taking distributions from these accounts for as long as possible would be ideal.

Now let's explore the Dinglehopper's options for generating income between age 55 and age 59 ½ (when they may begin to take distributions from their Rollover IRAs penalty-free). Rollover IRAs are out. Social Security isn't available. Roth IRAs could be accessed, as withdrawals of principal (as opposed to growth) would be tax-free despite not having reached age 59 ½. Nevertheless, as described earlier, it would be ideal to let the Roth IRAs grow unimpeded. What does this leave? Yes, indeed, the Dinglehoppers will need to rely on their investment account for survival until age 59 ½.

Now, just to add a little color to the Dinglehopper case study, imagine that they met with their investment advisor and determined that they would need net income (i.e., post-tax income) of approximately $95,000 per year to attain the standard of living they desire in retirement. Let's also imagine that their lovely primary residence is debt-free and they don't plan to sell it. We're going to discuss the rate of withdrawal in great detail later in this chapter, but for the sake of staying focused on our current scenario, we'll assume that the Dinglehopper's advisor ran a Monte Carlo simulation and accordingly reported that a 3 percent withdrawal rate from their overall portfolio balance (combined with Social Security in their later years, of course) would result in an extraordinarily high chance of not only carrying them all the way through their retirement years, but would also allow them to leave behind a meaningful inheritance for their two children.

Recall earlier that I said the Dinglehoppers investment account had only modest built-in capital gains. If they begin systematically liquidating positions inside their investment account to generate the $95,000 in annual net income they desire in the first four-plus years of retirement, their federal tax liability will be a big fat zero. Here's why: If we presume that my label of "modest" capital gains means that the $800,000 investment account carries $100,000 in long-term capital gains, we can quickly do some basic math to sort this out.

From a tax perspective, the Dinglehoppers are incentivized to initially focus on creating income by liquidating the winners in their portfolio, and accordingly, let's presume that they manage to take the entire existing gain of $100,000 prior to age 59 ½. Pro-rated across 4.5 years, this is $22,222 in gain per year. As a couple filing jointly in 2019, the Dinglehoppers won't pay a dime in federal capital gains tax until their combined income reaches $78,950.

Again, with an apology to my accountant friends for the oversimplified nature of this analysis, here is how the Dinglehopper's federal income tax burden would look if they simply proceeded by creating income in the following order: (a) withdrawing from the investment account, (b) withdrawing from their tax-deferred retirement accounts at age 59 ½, (c) taking Social

Security benefits at age seventy, and (d) withdrawing from their Roth accounts as required in their later years:

1. *Age 55 to 59 ½:* No federal tax liability of any kind.

2. *Age 59 ½ to 70:* Modest federal income tax liability on distributions from tax-deferred retirement accounts and potentially very modest capital gains tax liability associated with withdrawals from the investment account.

3. *Age 70 onward:* Moderate federal income tax liability on the combination of Social Security payments and distributions from tax-deferred retirement accounts and potentially modest capital gains tax liability associated with withdrawals from the investment account.

For those of you who appreciate tables, here is a high-level depiction of the different federal tax liabilities in graphic format. I'll use CGT as the acronym for capital gains tax and PIT as the acronym for personal income tax.

	Investment Accounts	Tax-Deferred Accounts	Social Security	Roth IRAs
Age 55 to 59 ½	No CGT	No PIT	No PIT	No PIT
Age 59 ½ to 70	Modest CGT	Moderate PIT	No PIT	No PIT
Age 70 onward	Modest CGT	High PIT*	High PIT*	No PIT

* This assumes that the Dinglehopper's tax-deferred accounts are invested sensibly and produce a reasonable return and accordingly result in large required minimum distributions.

My hope is that the chart illustrates a key point; namely, that the Dinglehopper's total tax liability will likely jump significantly as they move through the three stages of retirement. While a shoulder shrug and an *It is what it is* approach requires little work and won't be catastrophic for the Dinglehoppers, they have an opportunity to reduce their tax liability in a non-trivial manner by doing a bit of work with their advisor and accountant. In short, under the tax regime in place as of the writing of this book, the Dinglehoppers would benefit by capitalizing on their extremely lean tax profile in the early years of their retirement by converting some of their tax-deferred dollars into Roth dollars. Let's explore how this works, and then we'll return to the Dinglehopper example.

Roth Conversions. As a quick recap of a few retirement planning basics, all withdrawals from tax-deferred accounts are taxed at regular income tax rates at the time of withdrawal. There is no escaping this tax liability. Even if you pass away holding significant balances in your tax-deferred accounts, your beneficiaries will pay income tax on their withdrawals from these inherited accounts after your death. Conversely, if you begin withdrawing from a Roth IRA after age 59 ½, there will never be any income tax (or capital gains tax) associated with those withdrawals.

Under current rules, you are allowed to convert tax-deferred retirement account dollars into Roth dollars. This affords you an interesting opportunity to participate in a form of tax arbitrage (which is just a fancy way of describing saving tax dollars). Here's the catch: You will pay income tax on every tax-deferred dollar you convert to a Roth dollar. And here's the idea: You may be able to more easily absorb this tax liability in a year in which you otherwise don't have much regular income or capital gain to report.

Remember, we have a graduated income tax ladder, so it would seem a waste not to take advantage of the lower tax brackets while simultaneously limiting the taxation of retirement distributions in the future. Let's return to the Dinglehoppers to see how this works.

If the Dinglehoppers meet the totality of their retirement needs with withdrawals from tax-deferred retirement accounts and Social Security in the future, for the sake of simplicity let's assume they need roughly $110,000 per year from a combination of these sources to generate their required $95,000 in net income. After age seventy, roughly $73,000 of the required $110,000 in pre-tax income will be generated by Social Security payments. With me so far? Now hold on to your hats, because this is about to get funky.

Remember those pesky Required Minimum Distributions (RMDs)? Naturally, the more the Dinglehoppers have in their tax-deferred retirement accounts when they reach age 70 ½, the higher their RMDs. In fact, with their sizable tax-deferred retirement account balances of $1,700,000 at age fifty-five, if the market is kind and the Dinglehoppers accordingly don't significantly draw down their tax-deferred accounts prior to age 70 ½, the combination of Social Security and RMDs at age 70 ½ will push the Dinglehopper's total taxable income well above the roughly $110,000 in taxable income that they need. For example, if the Dinglehopper's tax-deferred account balances still total $1,700,000 at age 70 ½, their RMD might initially be around $62,000 per year. Combined with $73,000 in taxable Social Security income, and they are looking at $135,000 in taxable income. Worse yet, because of the manner in which RMDs are calculated, if the Dinglehopper's pre-tax retirement accounts are invested sensibly and market conditions are kind, these RMDs may continue to rise substantially.

Consider this: At a roughly 1 percent annual return, the Dinglehoppers RMDs would stay fairly constant for roughly twenty years at around $60,000 per year. But if they achieved an 8 percent annual return (crazier things have happened, certainly), the Dinglehopper's RMDs start to get mind-blowingly high (and would start climbing past $250,000 at age ninety). Just for fun, let's put on our rose-tinted glasses and imagine a 12 percent annual return. Now the Dinglehoppers are looking at an RMD of over $500,000 at age ninety, and it gets worse for the next decade. Needless to say, these RDMs generate an enormous tax liability.

So RMDs are scary… You understand that sentiment, I gather. The Dinglehoppers may be pushed to generate vastly more pre-tax income than they need. Hopefully the incentive to convert tax-deferred dollars into Roth dollars is more apparent. If not, I expect you to come to office hours after class.

Now, what happens when the Dinglehoppers actually start converting Rollover IRA balances into Roth IRA balances? They will pay income tax on the conversions, to be sure, but at potentially a significantly lower rate than they might face in their later years. Calculating exactly how much the Dinglehoppers should convert each year is a complex drill that involves some degree of speculation about the totality of their circumstances in the future (tax rates, investment return, etc.) Nevertheless, to pick a nice round number, converting

$100,000 per year from Rollover IRAs to Roth IRAs each year between ages fifty-five and fifty-nine might be sensible. This would shift $500,000 into the Dinglehopper's Roth IRAs and significantly reduce those scary RMDs to a level that is a bit closer to what they would actually require in retirement to generate the income they need.

Because I recognize that many of my readers are contemplating retiring early enough that they won't begin to immediately take distributions from their tax-deferred accounts (i.e., they are contemplating retirement prior to age 59 ½), I created the example of the Dinglehoppers to make it a bit easier to understand how "using up" those lower income tax rates through Roth conversions is beneficial in years that would otherwise result in no or little tax liability. It's not always so straightforward, of course.

Keep in mind that if you are receiving Medicare when you convert tax-deferred dollars into Roth dollars, you might be in for an unpleasant surprise. This is simply because your Medicare premium is tied to the amount of taxable income you reported in your most recent tax returns. For example, if you convert tax-deferred dollars to Roth dollars in 2020, your Medicare premium may increase in 2022. In addition, the amount of tax you pay on your Social Security benefit is also tied to your reported income, though if you are a higher-net-worth individual with healthy taxable income in retirement, 85 percent of your Social Security benefit will likely be taxed.

To simplify matters, here is a quick overview of several reasons you might want to contemplate converting some of your tax-deferred retirement dollars into Roth dollars:

1. You speculate (and it is indeed speculation) that your tax rate in your later retirement years will be higher than your current tax rate.

2. You don't anticipate that you will need to access your retirement funds until you are quite a bit older—i.e., you won't begin taking distributions from your Roth account shortly after converting funds.

3. You can pay the tax liability associated with the conversion using non-retirement funds.

4. You anticipate leaving a significant portion of your Roth IRA to your heirs and prefer that they receive funds tax-free.

The Fundamentals. Now that we've touched on Roth conversions and worked through an example of a couple who plan to retire at fifty-five and who are good candidates for using Roth conversion as a form of tax arbitrage, let's return to the fundamentals of creating income in retirement. How Roth IRAs function in retirement is easy to understand due to their post-tax nature. Tax-deferred retirement accounts require a bit more thought, in particular because of the impact that RDMs can have on your tax profile in retirement. In either case, though, the mechanism for creating income is clear. You simply sell some of the holdings inside the account (i.e., either voluntarily if it is a Roth, or involuntarily if it is a tax-deferred account and you in RDM territory) and withdraw the required cash from the account. Creating income from investment accounts is a bit more nuanced, as we will explore now.

When I discuss generating income in retirement out of a taxable account with my clients, I often encounter something I'll call the *dividend bias*. I have dealt with this time and again (not just with clients, but with immediate family members), and I find that it is just one of those things that people have a hard time digesting. Dividend bias is a preference for receiving dividends in lieu of creating income by incrementally liquidating a portion of a stock or fund holding. If I put on my therapist hat, I think this comes from the notion that it just *feels* different to have stock generate income (through dividends) v. having to actually sell a portion of the asset itself.

While I am one to celebrate the importance of feelings—remember the appetite for risk analysis we walked through earlier?—I don't want feelings to hamper your investment experience by causing you to structure a portfolio in an inefficient manner. If you are an investor who prefers to hold a series of stocks or funds in a portfolio that produce dividends, I'll do my best to persuade you to eliminate this bias. I'll point you toward plenty of good data to satisfy your analytical soul, but first, let's cover the basic truths that make the dividend bias problematic.

Nearly sixty years ago, Merton Miller and Franco Modigliani demonstrated that dividend policy isn't tied to stock returns in a paper titled "Dividend, Policy, Growth, and the Valuation of Shares." This analysis was validated time and again over the decades that followed publication. In short, stocks that have similar characteristics (size, value, profitability, etc.) have the same returns regardless of whether the stocks pay a dividend or not. Warren Buffet highlighted this fact when he announced a share buyback program for Berkshire Hathaway in 2011 in lieu of offering a cash dividend, and he nonetheless received some criticism for his decision to decline to offer a cash dividend.

Please understand that a dividend is offset by a reduction in the price of the underlying stock. Many investors seem to believe that somehow a company can offer a dividend and maintain the same stock price that would have applied had no divided been offered. This is simply not true and may be another example of magical thinking. There is no such thing as a free dividend.

The result of all of this? Selling off shares of a stock or fund—let's call this a *self-generated dividend*—initially looks very similar to receiving dividends. While generally this holds true, there are a few reasons that I prefer the self-generated dividend strategy for generating income in retirement: (a) taxation, and (b) diversification. I'll briefly address each.

Taxation. Long-term capital gains and qualified dividends are taxed at the same rates (i.e., preferential tax rates). Likewise, short-term capital gains and non-qualified dividends are taxed at the same rates (i.e., ordinary income tax rates). With that in mind, remember that capital gains tax is only payable on the portion of the sale of a security (or a fund) that represents gain. The rest is return of principal. Conversely, 100 percent of a dividend is taxable. Further, when using the self-generated dividend model, capital losses are a useful vehicle for offsetting gain. Said differently, with the self-generated dividend model, you can control your tax exposure to some degree. Not so with cash dividends.

Diversification. Roughly 60 percent of U.S. stocks do not pay a dividend. It doesn't take a great deal of imagination to understand why creating a portfolio that exclusively focuses on dividend-producing stocks is problematic if diversification is a priority.

If you've tracked this discussion, you may wonder why this dividend bias exists. Aren't humans supposed to act rationally?

Not by a long shot. We already know that humans are lousy investors, and while we should always theoretically act in our own best interests, the preference for dividends, which has persisted for decades despite significant evidence that this makes little sense, merely reinforces the notion that we are illogical creatures.

The behavioralists (champions of a particular school of economic thought) have tried to explain the origin of the dividend bias. Indeed, one reason for the dividend bias may be obvious. Many individuals struggle with disciplined spending. I can hear my grandfather's voice echoing in my head as I write this. *Don't touch the principal.* By restricting spending to cash generated by a particular stock or fund, we can be sure that we don't touch the principal… kind of. It *feels* that way, anyhow. The truth is that dividends are indeed tied to share price, so in my grandfather's language, it's really *six of one, half a dozen of the other.*

The other reason is less obvious, but will likely also become clear once we dig into the theory. *Loss aversion* is the name given to the endlessly tested idea that humans are loss averse. In other words, we value gains and losses differently, and we will go to great lengths to avoid losses, even if doing so doesn't make rational sense. Understanding how this applies to the self-generated v. cash dividend anomaly simply requires that we acknowledge that the self-generated dividend approach involves selling shares of stock or a fund. This can feel like a loss. Conversely, dividends feel like gravy. If you could avoid hitting the "sell" button and instead simply let the cash roll in, wouldn't that be nice? Well, not so fast. You now know that the share price of the underlying stock or fund is indeed impacted by the decision to issue a dividend. If you could *elect* to have a stock or mutual fund issue a dividend (certainly not the case for us mortals), you would simply be moving money from your left pocket to your right pocket. The problem is that you have less control over dividends than you do over the choice to sell shares.

The Rate of Withdrawal. At various points in this book, I've alluded to the importance of analyzing the rate of withdrawal from an investment portfolio and how it impacts financial health in retirement. I've also mentioned a "Monte Carlo analysis" several times. Well, we can't put this drill off any longer. Let's make sure you understand this important element of retirement planning. Though the topic is as dry as the Sonoran Desert in December, a Monte Carlo analysis may be your chief ally (along with a good advisor) in the quest to ensure your nest egg doesn't expire before you do.

To understand the value of a Monte Carlos analysis, first we need to acknowledge that most inconvenient facet of investing that drives some folks out of their minds with anxiety. Harnessing decent investment returns is a probability game. This is precisely why the older form of retirement planning, which assumed a constant rate of investment return (say, 7 percent), is problematic. While it's possible that a portfolio of stocks and bonds will produce an average return of 7 percent, it is certainly improbable (if not nearly impossible) that a basket of stocks and bonds will produce a return of 7 percent each and every year. Remember that volatility concept we analyzed earlier?

The beauty of a Monte Carlo analysis is that it uses (a) the average expected return of a portfolio, and (b) the standard deviation (i.e., volatility) of a portfolio to run tens of thousands of scenarios simulating the impact of a sequence of random returns. The result of a Monte Carlo analysis, properly presented, is a succinctly stated series of probabilities of achieving a certain result. Remember C3PO from Stars Wars, with his propensity for stating the odds of surviving various dangerous events (like flying through an asteroid belt)? Well, good ole' C3PO was running a series of calculations that are not unlike Monte Carlo simulations. Here are a few statements you might expect to come out of a Monte Carlo Analysis:

- There is a 93 percent chance that you will avoid depleting the balance of your portfolio in retirement.
- There is a 60 percent chance that your portfolio balance will rise to $4,500,000 as of the date of your death.
- There is a 10 percent chance that your portfolio balance will rise to $10,000,000 as of the date of your death.

The inputs into Monte Carlo software are critically important, of course. To obtain a reasonable result, the operator needs to think very carefully about the assumptions that are fed into the software. The variables that must be entered include age of the portfolio owner, the initial amount invested, the rate and timing of savings/contributions and withdrawals, the rate of inflation, and the volatility/return distribution of the portfolio. One of the great advantages provided by the software is the ability to test different assumptions with respect to asset allocation and withdrawal strategies.

So what do advisors do with the results of a Monte Carlo analysis? Well, among other things, it suddenly becomes much easier to quantify a clients' risk tolerance. Does a client blanche at the thought of a 75 percent chance of having his portfolio outlast his life? Is anything less than a 95 percent chance of success unacceptable?

Let's imagine that you have run through a Monte Carlo analysis and learned that you really don't need to take much risk to meet your income needs in retirement. In other words, you discovered that you have a significant chance (50 percent) of dying uber-wealthy if you maintain a portfolio of 70 percent equity and 30 percent fixed income and withdraw 4 percent annually from your portfolio. Further, you have a non-trivial 10 percent chance of running dry. Unless you harbor significant estate-planning-goals that require that you die with a huge nest egg, you may want to dial back the volatility in your portfolio by shifting the ratio of stock and fixed income significantly. Doing so will lessen the probability that you die uber-wealthy (perhaps to 10 percent) and will also lessen the chance that you run dry (perhaps to 2 percent).

Conversely, if you ran through a Monte Carlos analysis and learned that you need to assume an unacceptable level of risk to even have a chance of meeting your income needs in retirement, you are faced with a harder set of choices. You are forced to either (a) accept more risk than you are comfortable taking on, (b) save more, or (c) reduce your income needs in retirement—i.e., change your assumed withdrawal rate.

The relationship between your withdrawal rate, the allocation of assets within a portfolio, and the odds of success (defined as not outliving your investments as a probability) is illustrated in the table on the next page, which assumes a $1M starting portfolio balance, no additional contributions, and a thirty-year time horizon, with the calculated monthly withdrawal rate increased for inflation.

	3% withdrawal $2,500/mo	4% withdrawal $3,333/mo	5% withdrawal $4,167/mo
Portfolio A 75% stock 25% fixed income	99%	89%	66%
Portfolio B 50% stock 50% fixed income	99%	91%	54%
Portfolio C 25% stock 75% fixed income	99%	83%	16%

Your rate of withdrawal clearly has a significant impact on your ability to maintain an investment portfolio for the remainder of your lifetime. For the financially conservative investors among us, a modest withdrawal rate of 3 percent might be just the ticket, while those of us who are less concerned about leaving behind a legacy or running dry in our golden years might opt for a more aggressive withdrawal rate of 5 percent. Note, however, that if you opt for an aggressive withdrawal rate of 5 percent, you are best off with a portfolio with a significant stock allocation. If you opt for a conservative portfolio of only 25 percent stock and 75 percent fixed income (Portfolio C), your chances of making it thirty years are very slim indeed.

In summary, using software to run a Monte Carlos analysis is a great way to determine that right blend of (a) an acceptable amount of risk in your investment portfolio, and (b) an acceptable chance of achieving your goals. A first rough cut at analysis may leave you feeling quite satisfied that you are well-positioned to sail off into your retirement sunset, or it may leave you feeling that you need to either continue to save (and defer on retirement) or adjust your expectations in retirement.

CHAPTER 5

Other Assets

Real Estate

Fortunes have been made in real estate. Fortunes have been lost in real estate. Sounds a bit like the stock market, doesn't it? Folks who are wary about financial markets often feel much better about owning real estate. *It is real,* they will say. *I can touch it.* Challenging this thought pattern is as productive as discussing whether the Lamanites established an ancient civilization in South America in 600 BC with a Mormon missionary. It goes nowhere.

I am comforted by the fact that unless you have skipped ahead, you have made it through some challenging financial discussions, and your propensity for magical thinking may be limited. First, to understand how real estate behaves as an investment, we need to analyze those familiar old metrics, volatility and return. The experts at Zillow, Inc. have a keen interest in how real estate performs as an investment, and they have studied the subject at great length. For those of you who haven't heard of Zillow, it is the world's largest online database of real estate listing, among other things. What Zillow discovered, and perhaps isn't terribly surprising, is that returns and volatility in real estate are quite location sensitive. Said differently, real estate performs like very conservative bonds (say, short-term treasuries) in some locations and like small growth stocks in others.

Consider this: According to Zillow, between June 1, 2010 and March 1, 2020, real estate in Philadelphia, Pennsylvania has marched upward at a fairly consistent 1.98 percent per year.[xi] Conversely, real estate in Las Vegas has proven volatile, and after getting savaged in the mortgage crisis of 2008, home values have risen by a more impressive average of 6.8 percent from June 1, 2010 to March 1, 2020.[xii] Remember, risk and return are related, and real estate is a good example of this phenomenon.

But what about Palo Alto, California; Belleview, Washington; or Boulder, Colorado? Just like individual stocks, there are examples of local markets that have outperformed regional indices by a healthy margin for long periods of time. These, however, are the exception to the rule. In short, real estate tends to perform a lot like financial investments.

Now on to the important question: Does real estate have a place in an investment portfolio? To summarize using an intentionally ambivalent word: sure. Investing in a well-diversified publicly traded Real Estate Investment Trust (REIT) isn't a bad idea. Doing so offers a modest diversification benefit, as real estate and financial markets are *highly correlated*, as opposed to *perfectly correlated.* Remember what this means? While real estate and stock generally move in similar directions, they are just different enough to offer a bit of diversification benefit.

While I would certainly endorse allocating a modest percentage (say, 5 percent) of an investment portfolio to REITS, I urge you to think twice about investing directly in rental real estate. If acting as a landlord consistently proceeded smoothly and required no effort, rental real estate would be vastly more attractive as a component of a solid retirement plan. However, operating one or more rental properties as a source of retirement income isn't entirely unlike running a business. It is risky and requires more work than most folks realize.

If you rent out a granny unit attached to your primary residence to a trusted friend, relative, or a thoroughly vetted tenant, it may indeed be a winning proposition. The extra income is nice, and having someone capable and friendly nearby may be comforting. Buying a multi-unit building, on the other hand, or even purchasing a separate single-family home or condominium, may be an entirely different story.

Rental real estate comes with real baggage. Unlike publicly traded securities, bonds, mutual funds, etc., rental real estate suffers from a significant array of disadvantages: (a) the investment is not particularly liquid, (b) exiting the investment often comes with very significant costs, (c) it is hard to control the amount of income generated by the investment, (d) managing the investment can take considerable work, or if you prefer to pay someone else to manage it, can come at a considerable cost, (e) winding up with one or more deadbeat or destructive tenants can be financially devastating, and (f) in some markets, the threat of rent control risks stripping away much of the upside of your investment.

Now, more detail, because I know you are interested, right? First, a note about liquidity: A highly liquid asset is simply one you can sell quickly. Publicly traded stocks, most bonds, and shares of mutual funds and ETFs are examples of highly liquid assets. If you need funds in a pinch, you can sell the assets in a day or two. In a true seller's market, such as the San Francisco Bay Area for a significant portion of the twenty-first century, you may be able to unload your rental property fairly quickly (say, in 30-60 days). This isn't terrible. But keep in mind that in a true buyer's market, your listing may sit for months on end without a single bite. If you've asked tenants to leave the rental property in preparation for sale, you may be without rental income for many months. Cash starts to hemorrhage out of your designated rental checking account, and a sense of desperation creeps in. In short, a vacant rental property in a buyer's market, particularly if the property is subject to a mortgage note, starts to feel like quite a liability. In some instances, this leads to a fire sale, and a patient investor with deeper pockets than you reaps the benefit of your desperation.

Next, sales costs in the vast majority of real estate markets are exceptionally high. Countless articles have been written about this, and while in some instances a direct sale without enlisting the help of an agent is possible, don't count on it. In many counties, the selling party bears not only the fees charged by the seller's agent, but also the fees charged by the buyer's agent. Combined with closing costs, these expenses can easily reach five to 7 percent of the sales price of the home. To understand how devastating this can be, here's a simple example.

Hubert Harvey purchases a multi-unit building in Philadelphia for $1,000,000. He puts $200,000 down, and he takes out a mortgage note for the remaining $800,000. He owns the property for five years, during which time the value of his investment rises modestly. After dealing with a series of deadbeat tenants, which pushes his cash flow into negative territory, Hubert decides to sell the place. After sitting on the market for some time, the multi-unit building sells for $1,100,000. Realtor fees and closing costs are 7 percent, or $77,000. Hubert nets a profit of only $23,000, a total annual return of less than 2 percent on his initial $200,000 investment. In short, realtor fees gobbled up the vast majority of his return.

Now on to a word about income generation. Imagine that each of your investments contains a throttle. It could be a simple lever that allows you to control how much income your investment produces. A misinformed investor who suffers from the common dividend bias might have a lever with a few possible settings. He can shop around for stocks that produce larger or smaller dividends to control the income produced by his portfolio, but only to a degree. Remember, his dividend bias prevents him from actually selling shares of stock to generate income. Conversely, a sensible investor who understands the phenomenon of the self-directed annuity and simply sells the number of shares of stock or funds required to generate a target amount of income has a lever with an enormous array of possible settings, from full throttle (significant long-term capital gains) to neutral (no investment income). And finally, an investor who receives rental income from real estate has a rather clunky lever—*on* (rental income is flowing) or *off* (rental income is not flowing). This inability to control the nature and volume of income generated by residential real estate can have a significant tax disadvantage.

Lest you think that I unfairly discriminate against real estate, I should state for the record that I am a big advocate of owning your primary residence, and not only that, but I also want you to own it outright by the time you retire. This may seem contrary to my core belief that ideally financial decisions should be shaped by data, data, and more data. Indeed, if you are lucky enough to be locked into a mortgage note with a very modest interest rate, there is an extremely high probability that investing in stocks will generate a much higher return over time than the cost of your mortgage interest. Said differently, you may pay 4 percent on your mortgage note, but if you can earn an average return of 8 percent in the stock market, isn't there an easy answer here? Shouldn't you simply hang on to that mortgage, and instead of using your savings to pay it off, shouldn't you invest any available capital in the stock market?

While probability suggests that what I described should be a very good strategy, my answer is a soft no. I write "soft," because if you have lots of cash on hand, ample retirement and investment assets, and your existing mortgage note feel like a second thought, you may not be troubled by the fact that you still owe money on your house. For most of us, though, there are two big benefits that come with owning a house outright: (a) sleep, beautiful sleep, and (b) significant financial security.

The first of these two benefits is simply peace of mind. For you data-heads out there, this can be hard to quantify, but it does have value. The second of these two benefits is tied to the basic fact that once you own a house outright, it becomes an unusually secure asset in the event of a catastrophic turn of events. Not to be a fearmonger, but imagine that incredible unreimbursed medical bills have driven you to file for bankruptcy. Your home receives preferential treatment in bankruptcy proceedings. Your larger investment account does not.

Gold

When I speak with individuals who are adamant about investing in gold, I find that their ill-founded confidence in this particular investment is based in no small part on dystopian thought. Gold lovers might be survivalists, given the right geographic location, social circle, education, and degree of paranoia. Here's the idea: The federal government will unravel, our social support network will collapse, currency will become valueless, and hordes of hungry rioters wielding sawed-off shotguns will roam the charred remains of our once-mighty cities. We'll revert to a barter system, but somehow gold will be recognized as intrinsically valuable.

I'm exaggerating to make a point, of course. Described less absurdly, some investors view gold as a "safe haven" when financial markets are distressed, and they further argue that gold is a hedge against currency risk and the ever-present bogey of inflation. Let's analyze each of these in turn.

First, when a bear market in stock materializes, it is true that the price of gold suffers less than stock more often than not. According to a study by Claude Erb and Campbell Harvey in *The Financial Analysts Journal*, the authors found that the price of gold was stable or rose 83 percent of the time that stocks posted negative returns. This is to be expected, as gold is a miserable investment that has produced no real return for centuries. Wait, what? Yes, you heard me correctly, gentle reader. Gold has produced no real return for centuries.[xiii] With this track record, one would certainly hope that gold outperforms stock when markets tank. So is gold a safe haven? Kinda sorta, but a pretty terrible one.

Next, over extremely long time periods, gold does appear to hold its value (i.e., it is indeed a very long-term hedge against inflation). However, when measured over ten-year periods, Erb and Harvey found that the price of gold and inflation appear to be largely unrelated. In short, for the time horizons we care about when constructing retirement plans (ten years, twenty years, thirty years) gold is at best a questionable hedge against inflation. However, if we succeed in locating the ever-elusive Fountain of Youth in Florida, gold may indeed be a good hedge against inflation. To back this up, I refer you back to Erb and Harvey, who found that a Roman Centurion's pay (in gold, and adjusted for inflation) is basically the same as an Army Captain's pay today (again in gold).

Finally, Erb and Harvey found no evidence that gold is in fact a good hedge against currency risk. Said differently, changes in the price of gold are largely independent of shifting currency values. In other words, if the dollar weakens against the yen, there is no evidence that the price of gold will increase in any consistent way.

The takeaway? Gold may be useful for a few things (though surprisingly few), and it may look wonderful on that gangster-fabulous grill of yours, but it sure hasn't been a good investment, and while it is a relatively secure way to store value over an extremely long time horizon, you can do far better with a sensibly constructed portfolio of other investments.

Annuities

Ah yes, the annuity… Guaranteed income. Perfect security. Such a lovely concept, but the green pastures promised by investment advisors who peddle these investments are not the serene Swiss meadows featured in the Sound of Music. Not at all—instead, these pastures, while green at first glance, are riddled with landmines. Indeed, one reason (among many) that financial advisors have earned a bad rap is their unscrupulous insistence on peddling very expensive and very complicated annuities to unsuspecting clients. True, we all like financial security, and yes, we all like a good deal. A slippery annuity salesman will make it sound as if you are receiving exactly that when you purchase his favorite annuity, which is typically the annuity that pays the salesman the highest commission.

First, what is an annuity? It is a contract, simply put. You deliver a fixed amount of money to an insurance company (through a bank, investment company, insurance agent, or financial advisor), and in return, the insurance company promises to pay you a certain amount over a certain number of years (in some cases, your lifetime). In other words, if you aren't lucky enough to have earned a government or commercial pension, you can create roughly the same thing by ponying up enough cash. Some annuities are very easy to understand. Others are a mess. Let's start with the basic concept, and then we'll descend into the slippery world of complex annuities.

The Single-Premium Immediate Annuity (SPIA). An SPIA is a relatively straightforward financial instrument, and not surprisingly, this makes it the most appealing of all forms of annuities. Remember, always ask yourself this question before being sweet-talked into a complicated annuity scheme: Who benefits from the complexity? There is an easy answer, my friend, and it isn't *you*. Here's how the simplest form of a SPIA works. First, you deliver a lump sum of cash to an insurance company. Next, the insurance company promises you (or both you and your spouse) monthly incomes for the rest of your life (or both of your lives). Easy, right?

The amount of the payment you receive for the remainder of your life is dictated by two factors: (a) your age and life expectancy, and (b) interest rates. The first of these factors isn't hard to understand. The longer you live, the more the insurance company has to pay in total, and therefore both your age and your life expectancy significantly impact your payments. For example, a seventy-year-old male who purchases an annuity for $100,000 might expect to receive $547 per month, while a fifty-year-old healthy female who purchases an annuity for $100,000 might expect to receive $358 per month.

While the simplest form of SPIA involves consistent monthly payments for the remainder of your life, you can also choose to have your payments linked to the rate of inflation. In other words, to ensure that the purchasing power of your monthly payments remains the same, you can pay more up front in exchange for a promise that your payments will track inflation. In addition, it's important to know that you can purchase an annuity that covers not just your own life, but that of your spouse as well.

The Deferred-Income Annuity (DIA). A DIA is very much like an SPIA, only you don't start taking payments until a future date. For example, at age sixty you might purchase a DIA that doesn't start paying out until you reach age eighty-five. The DIA monthly payment may be over five times the payout of the SPIA. This makes sense, as lifetime annuities are all about mortality. Think of a DIA as a hedge against living a very long time. It is a form of old-age insurance, and a DIA can be a great tool for ensuring that you have the resources available to handle the cost of long-term care.

A very basic annuity (either a SPIA or a DIA) can be a fine investment, but my job is to ensure that you understand the pros and cons of sinking your hard-earned dollars into an annuity instead of a well-managed portfolio of stocks and bonds. Here are the compelling advantages associated with investing in a simple annuity:

(1) A Very High Level of Security. While it's possible that a particular insurance company will fail and jeopardize your annuity, if you pick an insurance company with a decent rating (more on that later), the probability that you will lose your annuity is very small. An annuity represents a secure and predictable source of retirement income, while the stock market offers absolutely no guarantee that you will be able to create a reasonable income stream from your investment returns. Said differently, an easy-to-understand annuity from a reputable insurance company offers an attractive "sleep-at-night" factor for those who are uneasy about financial markets.

(2) No Thought Required. Creating a reasonable income stream with a very basic annuity requires no thought. You come up with the required capital, and the insurance company promises you payments for the rest of your life. This makes financial planning considerably easier, and once you've decided on the scope of the annuity you'd like to purchase, there is an appealing "set it and forget it" factor.

Here are the disadvantages associated with investing in a simple annuity:

(1) The Legacy Factor. A simple annuity can be structured so that your spouse also receives lifetime payments (typically a very good idea) in the event that you pass away first. However, once the annuity has paid out, it has paid out.

There is nothing left for your other beneficiaries. If you wish to leave behind a significant sum for the next generation, investing a significant portion of your nest egg in a lifetime annuity is not a good strategy. By purchasing a large lifetime annuity, you are simply ensuring that the next generation will not have access to a significant portion of your net worth. This may not be terribly problematic in your case. For instance, if your children are all successful in their own right and financially independent, you may not be concerned about leaving behind a significant estate. However, if your children haven't been able to scrape together those ever-elusive down-payments to purchase homes, or if you have twelve grandchildren and you want to ensure that each and every one of them can afford to attend Stanford, a simple annuity may be a poor fit for you.

(2) <u>The Chump Factor</u>. Yes, if you purchase a lifetime annuity and pass away two weeks later, the joke is on you. But maybe you've already moved on to the next world at that point, so you won't be too worried about it. After all, to keep annuities affordable, some purchasers have to die prematurely.

(3) <u>Poor Return</u>. This one takes a bit of thought. If your life expectancy is 84 years, and you live to be 105, you have indeed received an excellent return on your investment. You won, and the life insurance company lost. That being said, the more important point is that the life insurance companies aren't calculating the payout on your annuity such that if you live precisely as long as expected, the return you receive is the return you might expect on a portfolio of stocks and bonds over a twenty-year period. Nothing of the sort. An SPIA is a conservative investment, both for you and for the life insurance company that underwrites it.

(4) Loss of Control. Once you purchase an annuity, you no longer have access to the capital you invested. True, you will receive monthly payments, but if you need a lump sum to pay unexpected medical bills, you are out of luck.

So how do you know if you would be a good candidate for purchasing an annuity, whether an SPIA or a DIA? If you meet most (or all) of the following criteria, an annuity might be a good fit.

- You are in good health.
- You have adequate savings to both purchase an annuity and maintain an emergency reserve fund.
- When presented with the possibility of choosing a more aggressive investment (stocks) or a less aggressive investment (bonds), you tend to opt for a less conservative investment.
- You highly value predictable, consistent income.
- You don't want to either (a) manage an investment portfolio on your own, or (b) hire a financial advisor to manage an investment portfolio on your behalf.
- You prioritize having a healthy income in retirement over leaving behind assets for the next generation.

Simple annuities like SPIAs and DIAs have become somewhat commoditized over the last decade, and the increase in competition among insurance companies has driven costs down. As a result, while I used to cringe whenever a client mentioned an annuity, if a client now expresses a preference for steady, low-risk retirement income and isn't worried about the considerable disadvantages I noted above, I will encourage my client to explore the possibility of purchasing a simple annuity. What I will never, ever do, however, is allow a client to venture down the almost universally misleading and costly path that is littered with creatively named, high-commission, poorly performing annuities.

If anyone ever tries to sell you something called a variable annuity with living-benefit guarantee, please run (don't walk) in the other direction. But the salesman made the annuity sound so sexy, you say! He described it as an investment with a guaranteed return but with a hedge against downside loss. He said I can't lose!

Screeeeeeeeeeech. That's the sound of me hitting the brakes on my Model T (no anti-lock brakes in those days). Did I just hear, "I can't lose?" Gentle reader, I will give you a gold star if you can recite the most important principle I've outlined in this book.

Risk and return are related!

Anyone who tells you an annuity can capture all of the glory of the stock market without any of the associated risk is trying to sell you the Brooklyn Bridge. Don't fall for it. Look them right in the eye, cross your arms, and say in your biggest voice, "Risk and return are related, fool!" Okay, maybe don't call him a fool, but at the very least you should gracefully excuse yourself.

I owe you at least a basic description of why these monstrosities are not for you. First, it's important to know that these annuities are sold as a "low-risk" hybrid investment that allows you to participate in the stock market but also provides you with guaranteed income. Truth be told, very few people who purchase these annuities actually understand them. Worse yet, the financial advisors and insurance agents who sell these annuities often don't understand them well either.

The annuity has two basic pieces: (1) a variable annuity, and (2) a guaranteed living-benefit rider. The variable annuity, unlike the boring (but effective) SPIAs and DIAs of the world, allows you to choose from a list of mutual accounts that hold a mixture of stocks and bonds. At first blush, this sounds interesting. After all, I cited "poor return" as a disadvantage of SPIAs and DIAs. Why not invest in the market? It's the fine print, of course. While the gain on the funds is tax-deferred, there is a surrender charge if you cancel the annuity within a specified number of years (often ten, but sometimes longer). The increased income/benefit base is not available for withdrawal. Instead, to collect any part of the gain, you are forced to annuitize the gain—i.e., turn it into lifetime monthly payments. This makes sense. It is an annuity after all, isn't it? Upon withdrawal, the funds you invested are taxed at ordinary income rates. Okay, a bit complicated, you think, but manageable. Where's the rub?

The second piece of the annuity is the guaranteed living-benefit rider. If your investment in the variable annuity is a belly flop—i.e., the underlying funds perform poorly—you still get a minimum guaranteed payout. Amazing! But wait, it gets more interesting. Your annuity has two stated values—an investment value and an income/benefit base. The investment value is the gain or loss in the mutual funds associated with the variable annuity, minus costs. The income/benefit base is the original investment you made, plus a guaranteed annual increase. Something like 5 percent might be typical for the guaranteed increase. And how does the exciting investment value concept work? If the mutual funds in your variable annuity outperform the minimum guaranteed annual increase, you get to add this amount to the income/benefit base. This all sounds pretty good.

But what if the market declines such that the mutual funds inside your variable annuity take a beating? Suddenly things look a little less rosy. Your guaranteed annual increase will still kick in, which is lovely. Unfortunately, though, to see any investment-value-driven future upward movement in your income/benefit base, the mutual funds inside your annuity will have to perform remarkably well. Not only will the funds have to increase in value by more than the prior loss, but they'll also have to increase in value by the amount of the guaranteed annual increase.

Confused? I'm not upset with you. Please be confused. This stuff *is* confusing. The takeaway from the preceding paragraphs is this: It is entirely likely that your wonderfully complex annuity will never do any better than the minimum guaranteed annual increase. In many cases, the "investment value" concept winds up feeling like an absolute fiction. You've simply paid a great deal more than you needed to in order to obtain an annuity with a guaranteed minimum annual increase. All of this leads me to my next topic: costs, costs, and more costs.

First, let's discuss that juicy sales commission, which is why that slick insurance agent appears to be foaming at the mouth as he tries to sell you a variable annuity with living benefit guarantee. A commission of 5 to 7 percent is typical. This is a non-trivial sum. Next, let's layer on the annual fees associated with the annuity. Even the leanest and most ethical financial institution imaginable (hello, Vanguard) feels that they need to charge a decent fee to cover the substantial overhead associated with managing the elements of this complex package—i.e., the annuity, the mutual funds, the death benefit (often applicable), and the income rider. While Vanguard might charge something like 1.75 percent, a typical insurance company will charge in excess of 3.5 percent for your annuity.

Suddenly that sexy investment value concept looks much less thrilling. If annual fees are 3.5 percent, and your guaranteed minimum annual increase is 5.0 percent, you will need to exceed an average annual return of over 8.5 percent to see your income/benefit base rise more than the guaranteed annual minimum amount. Well, an 8.5 percent annual increase has certainly been achievable over the years, I hear you say. I agree wholeheartedly, and this is why I find equities so compelling. Unfortunately, most of the sellers of annuities will require that you hold a sizeable portion of your investments in bonds. Combined with the fact that your choices of funds are limited, the chance of exceeding that required 8.5 percent annual increase starts to look less and less likely.

In the end, I hope the theme is clear. Unnecessary complexity simply means that someone other than you reaps the benefit associated with the layers of nonsense that surround fancy annuities. The insurance agent and the insurance company make out just fine. You don't.

Life Insurance

There is one fundamental idea about life insurance I want to drive home in this chapter. Here it comes:

Life insurance is a risk management tool, not an investment or retirement vehicle.

We'll explore the notion of using an insurance policy as an investment or retirement vehicle later, but first, let's analyze whether you should obtain a new policy (or continue to maintain your existing policy). To unravel this, there are two key questions:

Does *anyone* rely on you financially? and

Are your existing assets sufficient to allow your loved ones to maintain their standard of living after your death?

If your answer to the first question is no, you may not need insurance. While perhaps your love of a particular charity or organization may prompt you to maintain a policy so that you can leave behind a significant charitable legacy, if no one in particular relies on you for financial support, your hard-earned dollars are likely better spent elsewhere. If, however, you have (a) a spouse who relies on your income, (b) children who aren't yet self-supporting, (c) a close friend or relative who is struggling financially, purchasing a new life insurance policy or maintaining an existing policy may make good sense.

While the first question was fairly straightforward, I want you to think hard before you answer the second question. If you do have sufficient assets to allow your loved ones to maintain a reasonable standard of living for many years after your death, it's true that you may be effectively self-insured. Nonetheless, arriving at this conclusion should only follow a bit of analysis. Glancing at your investment account, noting the million-dollar balance, and then shouting, "Nope! We're good!" may leave your loved ones in a precarious position. Life is expensive. Review the section of this book on budgeting and create a realistic budget for your loved ones after your death. Leaving them in a position that requires them to aggressively draw down any remaining assets in your portfolio to survive is a bit harsh. On the other hand, if your existing portfolio of investments is sufficient to allow your loved ones to survive to age 120 on half of the expected return from the portfolio, you can safely skip the life insurance drill.

So what if you are nearing retirement, you are in good health, you have sufficient assets to maintain a reasonable lifestyle well into your late nineties, but you have two children who haven't yet "launched," and who may ultimately need assistance? A bit of cost-benefit analysis may be just the thing. What would it cost to obtain and maintain a term policy for five years? Does the death benefit payable to your not-yet-launched children merit the substantial premium? What about a cash-value policy that should eventually pay its own premium or one of those fancy-pants variable life policies that allow you to invest in a series of funds to obtain a better return? This stuff gets confusing. Ultimately, though, maintaining a policy for those beloved children of yours may be wise.

Before you wade into this intentionally confusing thicket, please be careful. Many a sly salesman will tout the incredible tax-avoidance possibilities associated with investing in a cash-value life insurance policy. Please plug your ears and chant "La la la!" at the top of your lungs when this sale pitch begins. Remember what I said about annuities? Complexity is not your friend. The same is true for life insurance. A straightforward term policy or guaranteed universal life policy may make good sense in your situation, but if you haven't yet purchased a cash-value policy, please don't. You can almost certainly do significantly better by investing in a well-diversified portfolio of stocks and bonds. To unravel the mystery of how life insurance policies work, you will first need a tutorial on the various flavors of life insurance.

Term life insurance. Though it can be used for other purposes, the basic intent of term life insurance is to replace lost wages in the event of death. Term life insurance has no cash-out value, and it is purchased for a fixed period (a "term"). Some term policies re-set annually (i.e., they have a one-year term) while others have longer level terms. Young parents often do well to purchase a twenty or thirty-year fixed-term policy. For the death benefit provided, term life insurance is typically relatively affordable for those who are in decent health.

No-lapse/guaranteed universal life insurance. This type of policy typically has little or no cash-out value, and it is typically purchased by older folks who want lifelong coverage.

Whole life insurance. This type of policy builds up cash value over time. In later years, the cash value can be used to keep paying the premiums. This type of policy is typically guaranteed for life, provided, of course, that the premiums are paid.

Universal life insurance. This is another flavor of cash-value policy, but it is *fancy* (read: not recommended by this particular advisor). And it comes in sub-flavors, just to make things more interesting. Plain old universal life insurance has a cash value that earns varying rates of interest. Variable universal life insurance has a cash value that is invested in a variety of mutual funds. Indexed universal life insurance has a cash value that is loosely (cough, cough) linked to the stock market.

Unlike those halcyon days when you carefully picked your favorite ice cream flavor at the local Baskin Robbins, you won't be faced with choosing from thirty-one flavors of life insurance, but it can feel that way. Each client's life circumstances are unique, and a one-size-fits-all strategy can run the risk of fitting poorly. Nonetheless, here is some quick guidance in the interest of stopping that reflexive, boredom-induced head-nodding you're doing.

- If you're under sixty and in reasonably good health and you don't need lifetime coverage, consider term life insurance.

- If you're over sixty and you need lifetime coverage, consider no-lapse/guaranteed universal life insurance.

- If you want to be bamboozled by nonsense and fund the new purchase of an automobile for your insurance agent, consider variable universal life insurance.

I realize I risk offending some of you with my sarcastic comments about variable universal life insurance. I'm sorry. But, like the Marines used to say, "I never promised you a rose garden." So what do you do if you already own one or more cash-value policies? First, be kind to yourself. This is not a disaster. And also, please don't burn your life insurance agent with a negative online review. It's entirely possible that your agent (a) picked a policy that is indeed appropriate for you, (b) did an excellent job of explaining the ins-and-outs of your sub-optimal policy to you, or (c) sold you a junky policy, but simply didn't know any better—i.e., the sad, but all too common, innocent agent excuse.

If you currently hold a whole life policy (the simple flavor of cash-value policy), you may be paying a fixed premium each and every year. In the alternative, it's possible that you chose to pay high premiums during the policy's early years so that the policy will be fully paid-up by the time you reach, say, age sixty-five. Let's keep this simple. If you have determined that you no longer need life insurance, you can cancel the policy and collect the cash value. If you have determined that you still need life insurance and the policy is fully paid-up, I would suggest that you simply hold on to the policy (duh). And if you have determined that you still need life insurance, but the policy isn't fully paid-up and you no longer want to pay premiums, I would suggest exploring whether or not you can use the cash value of your whole life policy to fund a smaller, fully paid-up policy from the same insurer.

If you currently hold a cash-value universal life insurance policy of some kind, please be aware that it can be extremely difficult to decipher how to get the most bang for your proverbial buck with the policy you hold. I suggest that you try to find a good, fee-only insurance advisor to walk you through your options. Generally speaking, if your policy is performing miserably as an investment vehicle (entirely possible), you can cancel the policy and collect the cash surrender value. Be careful, though, about the timing of your request. Most policies come with a surrender charge if you cancel the policy before a certain date. Naturally, if you are close to the date upon which the surrender charge expires, hold off on canceling the policy until you can do so without a surrender charge.

Of course, just as you can with a whole life policy, if you have determined that you still need life insurance, but the cash-value universal life insurance policy isn't fully paid-up and you no longer want to pay premiums, you might be able to use the cash value to purchase a smaller, fully paid-up policy from the same insurer. If you're in reasonably good health, you might also consider canceling the policy and purchasing a smaller, no-lapse/guaranteed universal policy from another company in a tax-free exchange.

Before you cancel your existing policy and collect the cash value, I suggest that you explore the possibility of whether an investor might pay more for your policy than the cash value. Wait—what? This sounds awfully strange, doesn't it? Remember, this whole investing thing is an exercise in probability, and while your death is a certainty (sorry, my friend), exactly when you die is a roll of the dice. If (a) your health isn't great, and it looks like you have less than ten years to live, and (b) the death benefit of your policy is over $250,000, it's possible that an investor will be interested in purchasing your policy. For those of you who enjoyed watching the Simpsons, you can easily imagine old Mr. Burns (the nuclear-power-plant-owning town millionaire) rubbing his hands together gleefully at the thought of your premature death and the fantastic return he will receive on his rather morbid investment. Anyway, if you want to ditch your policy and you satisfy the criteria set forth above, an insurance agent should be able to help you find a so-called "life settlement broker." You can also check out LISA.org, which lists the members of the Life Insurance Settlement Association.

CHAPTER 6

Legacy Planning

In my years as an estate-planning attorney, one immutable truth came up time and again. One of the greatest gifts you can leave your loved ones is a carefully constructed estate plan. In other words, passing significant assets to your beneficiaries is nice. Leaving those assets to your beneficiaries in a carefully structured manner is much, much nicer. If you have already met with an estate-planning attorney and created a strong estate plan, please skip this section. If you are one of the millions of well-to-do individuals who have devoted a great deal of effort to accumulating assets but haven't spent more than a few minutes thinking about what will happen when you die, read on.

Dying Without an Estate Plan

By default, far too many individuals opt in to the "do nothing" approach to estate planning. This results in what is known as "intestate succession." In two words, intestate succession is *no bueno*. It means you are subscribing to the default inheritance rules established in your state of residence, which generally provide for your spouse and/or children. If you have no spouse or children, the probate court will typically leave your assets to your parents or siblings, or if you don't have any, to your cousins, aunts, uncles, nieces, nephews, etc. Intestate succession requires that your estate go through probate (more on that later), and if you have children, your children will receive 100 percent of their share of your estate the day they turn eighteen. See any problem with this? If you're with me, I'll assume that you will actually take the time required to establish an estate plan and move on.

Elements of an Estate Plan

Before I dive into a description of the basic elements of an estate plan, let me get something out of the way. Estate planning in the United States is governed by absurd, antiquated English law. Okay, I said it. Englishmen, before you set your hunting hounds on me, please keep in mind that I am a bit of an Anglophile in many respects. Just not in this one. Trust law is ridonculous (sic), and competes with the early tortured writing of Thomas Aquinas when it comes to confounding logic and questionable utility.

Living Trust. So what is this nutty idea? By creating a revocable living trust during her lifetime, a trustor (or "settlor" or "person establishing a trust") removes assets from her probate estate (or "assets that are subjected to a long, public, and expensive process known as probate"). Probate = bad, ergo, living trust = good.

Okay, so a properly funded living trust (more on this later) dodges probate. Sounds lovely. So what is a living trust, exactly? Can you touch it? Well, kind of, but only in the sense that a living trust is created by a document. A living trust is really a concept. It's a thoroughly British construct that you need to embrace (if you haven't already) in order to spare your loved ones considerable additional pain when you kick the bucket. Sound sensible? If so, dust off your powdered wig and break out the tea set, as you truly are an Anglophile.

The bulk of your assets should be contributed to your trust through the process of retitling assets, also known as "funding" your trust. In short, to fund your trust, you would typically retitle the following assets (among others) into your name as trustee of your trust: your real estate (by filing a new deed at the County

Recorder's office), investment accounts (by retitling accounts with the help of your investment advisor), and cash accounts (by going to the bank and retitling accounts). Each state has a threshold for assets that can be left outside of a trust without triggering probate. In California, this amount is $150,000. Said differently, if you live in California, you can leave a checking account with a $150,000 balance outside of your trust without triggering a probate proceeding, so long as you don't have other probate assets that would push you above this limit. Of course, it is best to play it safe and self-impose a lower threshold when structuring your estate plan. For example, ensuring that you have less than $100,000 in cash accounts outside of your trust is a sensible strategy.

While you are alive, you can do anything you want with the assets in your trust. You can sell the assets, borrow against them, or take them out of your trust. Further, so long as you have mental capacity, you are nearly always the initial trustee of your own living trust. In other words, *you* (trustee) manage the assets inside your revocable trust for *you* (trustor). Once you die, your living trust becomes irrevocable (meaning the terms can't be changed), and then your successor trustee manages your estate and either delivers assets directly to your beneficiaries or holds assets in further trust for your beneficiaries. Did you get that last bit? Upon your death, it wouldn't be unusual for your trust to split into a number of sub-trusts—one for each of your children. Your successor trustee would then manage each sub-trust until the final distribution is completed and the last remaining sub-trust can be terminated.

Pour-Over Will. Now let's imagine that you moved the bulk of your estate into your living trust by appropriately retitling assets. Well, then, when you die, what happens to the assets that you left *outside* of your trust? These aren't trust assets, after all. Are you ready for some tortured logic? Brace thyself, young scholar. In addition to a trust, you need a pour-over will. Think of the pour-over will as a lapdog (we'll call him Buttercup) and a living trust as the Lord of the Manor (we'll call him Lord Trust). Upon your death, Buttercup races about and fetches all of the assets that were left outside of the reach of Lord Trust and then dumps these assets in his lap. In other words, the pour-over will is simply the vehicle that ensures that all assets are ultimately distributed according to the terms of the trust after death.

Do you follow? For once, I'm not sure if *yes* or *no* is the better answer. If you don't really get it, no office hours are required. I'll let it slide this time, and you'll still get a passing grade. That being said, I hope you understand that a living trust and a pour-over will are both key ingredients of an estate plan. Sadly, it doesn't stop there. You will also need a durable financial power of attorney and a health care directive or living will, among other things.

Durable Financial Power of Attorney. The successor trustee of your living trust typically has the authority to step in and manage your trust assets in the event that you are incapacitated. After all, a living trust is a "real" mechanism prior to your death. But remember those non-trust assets we just discussed? Your pour-over will doesn't take effect until you die. In other words, in the event of your incapacity, the assets outside your trust appear to be just sitting there, lonely and unmanaged. But did our crusty, white-wigged barrister forefathers think of this? Of course they did! The durable power of attorney saves the day. Your agent (i.e., the person you appoint to manage your financial affairs) under your durable power of attorney, has the authority to manage your assets in the event that you are incapacitated.

Health Care Directive and/or Living Will. A health care directive and/or living will (depending on your state of residency) allow you to appoint an agent to make important medical decisions on your behalf in the event that you are incapacitated. This is an incredibly important document for a host of reasons, including the stressful but all-important end-of-life decisions that too few of us think about. A HIPAA (Health Insurance Portability Accountability Act) Release goes hand-in-hand with a health care directive and simply allows a physician to release medical information to the agent specified in the health care directive.

The Fundamental Questions

Selecting Successor Trustees. The importance of naming several competent successor trustees to manage the distribution of your estate following your death can't be over-stated. Think of your successor trustee as the CEO of your estate. While the successor trustee often has the authority to retain a helper of one kind or another (a "special agent," such as an accountant) to manage your estate, the authority of the successor trustee and significance of her role shouldn't be overlooked. If you are married, typically your spouse will act as the successor trustee of your estate. If you don't have a spouse, or you and your spouse die simultaneously, your successor trustee can be a child, other relative, friend, or financial institution ("corporate trustee").

For some individuals, picking a successor trustee merits little thought. Maybe it's a trusted sibling or a child who is sufficiently old to accept the responsibility that may come with the position. For others, deciding who will act as a successor trustee is a stressful ordeal. If you find that you don't have any living relatives who are willing or able to act as your successor trustee, working through a list of friends or acquaintances to determine who is qualified and willing to do the job can be daunting.

When selecting successor trustees, I would suggest that you pick two alternates, meaning that if your first choice can't or won't accept the position, a second choice is contacted, and then if necessary, a third. Trustworthiness is certainly the most important quality in a successor trustee, simply because it is critical that you are confident that your trustee will carry out your wishes to the best of his ability. Financial acumen is also high on the list of desirable qualities, as a trustee may need to work closely with a financial advisor or accountant to manage continuing trusts. A measured, rational personality is also highly desirable, as is the ability to get along with beneficiaries. Remember, if you pass away while your children are young and elect to defer distributions from your estate to your children until they are well into their twenties or thirties, the trustee may have a decades-long relationship with your children.

Beneficiaries: Who are They, and How Much Should They Receive? For the majority of clients who create an estate plan, the question of who should ultimately benefit from the plan is an easy one—children and grandchildren. If you enjoy a good relationship with each of your children and/or grandchildren, and each of them is healthy and responsible, count your blessings. This next section will be fairly straightforward. If one or more of your children and/or grandchildren has developed a dangerous habit (drug or alcohol addiction) or has significant special needs, please promptly make your way to the offices of a skilled estate-planning attorney, as you'll need to put quite a bit of thought into your estate plan.

Minor Children. Clients with young children simply don't know whether their children will grow into responsible adults. Unfortunately, devoting every effort to raising a responsible child is no guarantee of success, and in some instances, an estate plan will need to be modified as the children age into adulthood and beyond. Nevertheless, most clients with minor children understandably assume that the passage into adulthood is a smooth one, and they plan accordingly.

The question of how much to leave to each child is challenging for many clients. What will the kids do with what they receive? Will a sizable inheritance prevent them from working hard? Will the children manage their inheritance well, or will they blow through it at an alarming rate by purchasing Maseratis, yachts, timeshares, and jewelry? Though there are many contrary examples (and generalizing has limited utility), clients who haven't yet crossed the threshold of immense wealth (perhaps something like $10 million in assets) often leave everything to their children, while clients with immense wealth often divide their estates between charitable beneficiaries and children. No two families share the same dynamic, and different value systems may dictate vastly different approaches to structuring distributions from an estate. Nonetheless, once the total share each child is to receive has been established, exactly when each share should be distributed merits thought. In other words, should each child receive all of his or her share at age eighteen? Age twenty-five? Age forty? What about the needs of the child while he or she is a minor? And what about college costs?

Nearly every client with whom I have worked agrees that the trustee of a trust established for a minor child (more on this important position later) should retain the authority to distribute trust funds for the child's education. This is typically expanded to include the authority to distribute funds for a child's health, education, maintenance, and support. In other words, a trustee almost universally has the authority to dip into a child's share of the estate to pay for college tuition, housing costs, or unreimbursed medical costs.

A typical estate plan will then instruct the trustee to deliver the remainder of a child's estate to the child at defined ages. This is often referred to as "tiered distribution." Remember, if a client has young children when initially creating an estate plan, we can't be sure how the kiddos will turn out. Will Little Suzy grow into a pediatric surgeon who spends a month each year revising cleft palates in an impoverished country, or will she be a "social media influencer" who spends her days taking selfies, buying handbags, and snorting her inheritance up her nose? Will Little Suzy be able to manage a sizable sum at age twenty-five, or would it be best to mitigate risk by distributing her inheritance to her in three stages over a period of ten years?

Facing the unknown, many clients will opt for three-tiered distribution. Imagine that Little Suzy Q is eight years old, she has a twelve-year-old brother, and Mr. and Mrs. Q have accumulated roughly $4.2 million in assets. The Qs opt to treat their children equally (generally a wise strategy), and accordingly, when Mr. and Mrs. Q tragically perish in an automobile accident, their estate is immediately divided into two shares. The Qs's trust further dictates that Suzy's $2.1 million share should be delivered to her as follows: After college and other costs have been paid out of Suzy's share, she is to receive one-third (1/3) of the remaining funds in her trust at age twenty-five, one-third (1/3) at thirty, and one-third (1/3) at thirty-five.

While the Qs naturally hoped that Suzy would be able to manage the remainder of her share of the estate at age twenty-five, here is what they envisioned:

1. First, the trustee would help cover basic living expenses when the children went to live with Mrs. Q's sister (who was duly appointed guardian for the children). They anticipated that this could require approximately $100,000 from Suzy's share of the estate.

2. Next, the trustee would pay for college tuition, room and board, and basic living expenses while Suzy obtained an

undergraduate degree. They anticipated that this could require another $200,000 from Suzy's share of the estate.

3. When Suzy turns twenty-five, the Qs conservatively anticipated that Suzy would make a series of financially poor choices with her one-third (1/3) distribution of the remainder, which would be approximately $600,000. Maybe Suzy would spend it traveling the world or launching and then shuttering an ill-thought-out business. Maybe Suzy would buy expensive stuff that depreciates like crazy—a luxury car, a boat—or simply live dramatically beyond her means. Or maybe Suzy would entrust the first distribution of her trust to a friend who invests it all in a new form of cryptocurrency. Simply put, Mr. and Mrs. Q conservatively assumed that Suzy would blow through her first distribution. Even good children can make poor choices when suddenly presented with a sizable amount of cash.

4. When Suzy turns thirty, Mr. and Mrs. Q assumed that Suzy's experience at age twenty-five would be fresh in her memory. While Suzy might spend more than she should on expensive vacations, rather than blow through the next $600,000, maybe Suzy would use a large share of the distribution for a down-payment on a house.

5. When Suzy turns thirty-five, Mr. and Mrs. Q speculate that Suzy may have started a family of her own. Ideally, she will guard the final $600,000 fiercely, and invest wisely with an eye toward sending her own children to college and/or amassing a decent nest egg for retirement.

In short, Mr. and Mrs. Q wanted to ensure that their children had three chances to make a financially prudent choice with their inheritance. Not knowing exactly how the kiddos would turn out, it felt like a good way to hedge against poor choices made early in life. The three-tiered strategy employed by the Qs does typically work well for clients, though there are clear (and glaring) exceptions.

If you are contemplating deferring a distribution beyond age thirty-five for a child, a word of caution: Doing so can create a great deal of resentment. As an estate planner, I have often worked with the adult beneficiaries of estates. While presumably parents mean well when they don't allow a child to touch an estate until age forty (or worse yet, fifty), the inferred message to the child is clear. *We don't trust you.* While there is certainly no right answer on this issue, if a child is a screw-up at age thirty-five, there is a very reasonable chance she will still be a screw-up at age forty. In other words, the value of deferring a distribution for another five years may be questionable. Conversely, to a child who becomes a pediatric surgeon and desperately wants to purchase a house in an insanely expensive market (such as the San Francisco Bay Area), deferring that critical down-payment for another five years can be painful indeed.

Adult Children. If you have adult children, creating a sensible estate plan may be a bit easier. After all, presumably you have some sense of who your children have become as fully grown humans. It may be that your son is an incredibly frugal musician who plays with the New York Philharmonic, consistently demonstrates a great deal of financial acuity, and who will have no problem managing the entirety of his share of your estate at age twenty-five. Conversely, it may be that your daughter is a "spendthrift" (the antiquated term for someone who spends like crazy) and suffers from drug addiction and will need an endless series of very small distributions from your estate.

While my examples above may dictate treating children differently, please be very cautious with this concept. In my experience, only a truly dire set of circumstances (such as substance abuse, mental illness, etc.) merits treating children differently. Please think very carefully about the implications of this strategy before you divide your estate unequally between children. Often this strategy initially appears sensible. Perhaps Suzy, a senior executive at a pharmaceutical company, has already amassed millions of her own, while Johnny, an elementary school teacher, doesn't have a nickel to his name. Distributing $3 million to Johnny and $1 million to Suzy may seem like the right thing to do—after all, Johnny needs the cash more than Suzy—but the message delivered to Suzy with such an unequal distribution can be devastating. Suzy may feel that she was punished for doing well. Treating children differently in an estate plan can create palpable strain in the dynamic between surviving siblings, and resentments can quickly develop. Better to give Suzy half of the estate, and if she feels it is appropriate, she can decide to deliver a portion of her share to her brother. This way Suzy feels that she was treated equally, and further, she will receive the emotional credit that comes with deciding that her brother needs additional help.

Another word of caution when creating an estate plan if you not only have adult children, but also grandchildren: Please be careful not to over-step your children's parental authority. While setting aside funds for the grandchildren's education seems to be almost universally appreciated by children, I encourage most clients to shy away from leaving additional assets directly to grandchildren. Doing so can feel quite controlling and may convey distrust. Instead, passing your wealth down one generation and then leaving it to your children to provide for the grandchildren sends a nice message. It conveys a sense of trust, while also honoring what is usually true—children will guide grandchildren into adulthood and will have the capacity to plan more carefully for the grandchildren's benefit.

Charitable Beneficiaries. There are a number of estate-planning techniques available for clients who are charitably inclined, and exploring each and every one of them is beyond the scope of this book. Beyond simply naming a charity as a beneficiary of an estate, options for delivering assets to charitable organizations include the use of Donor Advised Funds (DAFs), charitable lead trusts, and charitable remainder trusts. If charitable giving will be a significant part of your financial plan and estate plan, I suggest that you choose a financial advisor who is familiar with the tax and other implications of charitable giving and can work with an estate planner who likewise has deep knowledge of the field.

In the event that you decline to meet with an advisor with expertise in charitable giving, I want you to at least be aware of two important tax principles that should shape how you structure gifts to charities while you are still living: (1) when in doubt, donate highly appreciated assets, and (2) consider donating to charity from tax-deferred retirement accounts such as IRAs after age 70 ½.

To understand why donating highly appreciated assets instead of cash is wise, please recall that capital gains tax is payable on the difference between what you paid for the asset (the basis) and the sales price (the fair market value). Imagine that you decided to sell 1,000 shares of Gizmo, Inc. stock at $100 per share (i.e., a total of $100,000) and donate the resulting cash to charity. Further, assume you had bought the stock at $10 per share (i.e., a total of $10,000). You would be required to pay capital gains tax on the $90,000 gain. Conversely, if you donated the shares of Gizmo, Inc. stock to a charity (perhaps through a Donor Advised Fund), you would face no capital gains tax, and you could fully deduct the donation over a period of years.

Remember the earlier analysis of Required Minimum Distributions (RMDs) and how they can drive your tax rate into the stratosphere in retirement if you don't do a bit of careful tax planning? No? Well, I don't entirely blame you, as it's been quite a few pages since then. Nonetheless, I'll keep it simple. If you have accumulated significant pre-tax retirement account balances (say, in one or more IRAs) and you continue to invest prudently, your RMDs may be taxed quite heavily. As a result, you may want to consider achieving your charitable goals by using what are called Qualified Charitable Distributions (QCDs) from your IRAs. This has a few benefits: (a) the QCDs are not reported as income on your tax returns, and (b) you can still use the standard deduction—i.e., the QCDs are not considered itemized deductions, and (c) if your RMDs are sizable, the QCDs will dodge what would otherwise be a fairly sizeable 3.8 percent Net Investment Income Tax on the amount donated.

Too technical? Yeah, I hear you, compadre. Just file the basics away in that head of yours. If you are charitably inclined and want to reduce the tax burden on your RMDs, consider QCDs. And if your advisor stares blankly back at your when you mention QCDs, perhaps you should shop around for someone who has more retirement planning experience.

Parting Thoughts

Well, you did it. I only caught you sleeping a few times, which isn't too bad. Are you ready for your final exam?

Okay, here it is. I want you to fill in the missing word in the following sentences:

1. Risk and return are _____.
2. Believing that we can consistently outsmart the market is an example of _____ thinking. (Hint: think Harry Potter).
3. Volatility has a _____ impact on the return of a portfolio.
4. Owning a home offers many individuals sufficient inclusion of ______ in their investment portfolio.
5. One of the primary goals of establishing a living trust is to ensure that your beneficiaries avoid the time-consuming, costly court process known as ______.
6. Short-term capital gains are taxed at ______ tax rates.
7. The dividend _____ states that dividends can not be distributed to shareholders without an impact on share price.
8. There is no such thing as a free _____ (except at IKEA, where you can get a hot dog and frozen yogurt for $1.75, which is almost free).
9. A Roth _____ allows you to create a Roth IRA by paying all of the income tax due on a Traditional or Rollover IRA.
10. The author of this book has a _____ sense of humor.

Answers:

1. related
2. magical
3. negative
4. real estate
5. probate
6. regular or "regular income"
7. fallacy
8. lunch
9. conversion
10. acceptable answers: terrible, ridiculous, silly, lame, goofy, absurd, juvenile, bad, dumb

I grade students on a generous curve, so here's the deal. If you scored ten out of ten correct, you get an A+. You can cut off the cover of this book, mail it to me after autographing it with a handwritten note, and I will respond with a coupon for a free scoop of Baskin Robbins ice cream. Just don't order the bubblegum flavor. Don't say I didn't warn you.

If you scored nine correct, you get an A. If you scored eight correct, you get an A-. Seven correct, a B+. Six correct, a C. Five or fewer correct, you fail. And if you failed, I weep for you (for the time you wasted on this book), but I will hold out hope that your talents shine brightly in other disciplines.

APPENDIX

Sample Budget

Below you will find a detailed budget for Linda, a retired tech executive with a relatively high cash-flow requirement in her retirement years. Linda contemplates maintaining two homes—a primary residence and a much smaller vacation cottage—and she also plans to travel frequently. Both homes are paid off in full, and Linda carries no debt of any kind.

Category of Expense	Monthly Cost
Housing:	
Property Tax (Primary Residence)	$1,500
Property Tax (Vacation Home)	$400
Homeowner's Insurance (Primary Residence)	$190
Homeowner's Insurance (Vacation Home)	$80
Cable TV and Internet (Primary Residence)	$150
Cable TV and Internet (Vacation Home)	$90
Landscaping (Primary Residence)	$200
Weekly Cleaning (Primary Residence)	$250
Periodic Cleaning (Vacation Home)	$100
Maintenance and Repair (Primary Residence)	$600
Maintenance and Repair (Vacation Home)	$200
Total Housing Expenses	*$3,760*

Automobile:	
Insurance and Registration	$110
Gas	$100
Maintenance and Repair	$200
Total Automobile Expenses	*$410*
Groceries and Sundries:	
Groceries	$750
Drug Store (Sundries)	$120
Total Groceries and Sundries	*$870*
Personal Grooming:	
Hair salon	$35
Nail salon	$20
Skin care/Dermatologist	$50
Total Personal Grooming	*$105*
Clothing:	
Clothes	$180
Shoes	$40
Total Clothing Expenses	*$220*

Medical Premium:	*$350*
Unreimbursed Medical & Dental Expenses:	
Dental Care	$60
Prescriptions	$20
Eye Glasses	$10
Chiropractor	$60
Medical Co-Pays	$100
Total Unreimbursed Medical & Dental	*$250*
Entertainment:	
Streaming Video (Movies at Home)	$20
Movies at the Theater	$40
Opera Season Tickets	$150
Eating Out	$400
Books	$35
Total Entertainment	*$645*
Travel:	
Round-Trip Airfare (Three Trips Per Year)	$360
Hotels	$500

Ride-Share/Cabs	$20
Total Travel	*$880*
Gym Membership:	*$120*
Gifts (Birthdays and Holidays):	*$80*
Misc.	*$200*
Grand Total	***$7,890***

NOTES

[i] Fidelity. (2020, August 3). *How to Plan for Rising Health Care Costs.* https://www.fidelity.com/viewpoints/personal-finance/plan-for-rising-health-care-costs

[ii] Kaiser Family Foundation. (2014, January 9). *Health Care on a Budget: The Financial Burden of Health Spending by Medicare Households.* https://www.kff.org/medicare/issue-brief/health-care-on-a-budget-the-financial-burden-of-health-spending-by-medicare-households

[iii] Metlife Mature Market Institute Market Survey of Long-Term Care Costs.

[iv] FTSE Russell. (n.d.). *Frequently Asked Questions.* Retrieved June 5, 2019, from https://www.ftserussell.com/research-insights/russell-reconstitution/reconstitution-frequently-asked-questions

[v] Kinniry Jr., Jaconetti, DiJoseph, Zilbering, & Bennyhoff. (2019, February). *Putting a Value on Your Value: Quantifying Vanguard Advisor's Alpha.* https://www.vanguard.com/pdf/ISGQVAA.pdf

[vi] Sass, S. (1997). *The Promise of Private Pensions: The First Hundred Years,* at 54.

[vii] Wiatrowski, W. (2001, April). *Changing retirement age: ups and downs. Laws and research, United States —Statistical Data Included, Monthly Labor Review.* http://www.bls.gov/opub/mlr/2001/04/art1full.pdf.

[viii] Employee Benefits Research Institute. (1998). *History of Pension Plans.* http://www.ebri.org/publications/facts/index.cfm?fa=0398afact.

[ix] Employee Benefits Research Institute. (1998). *History of Pension Plans.* http://www.ebri.org/publications/facts/index.cfm?fa=0398afact.

---

[x] U.S. Department of Labor, Bureau of Labor Statistics. (2018, March). *National Compensation Survey: Employee Benefits in the United States*, Private Industry Tables, Table 2.

[xi] Zillow. (n.d.). $148,700 median price on June 1, 2010 and $185,700 median price on March 1, 2020. Retrieved May 6, 2020 from Zillow.com

[xii] Zillow. (n.d.) $144,300 median price on June 1, 2010 and $290,500 median price on March 1, 2020. Retrieved May 6, 2020 from Zillow.com

[xiii] Bredin, D., Thomas C., and Poti, V. (2014). Does Gold Glitter in the Long-Run? Gold as a Hedge and Safe Haven Across Time and Investment Horizon. *International Review of Financial Analysis*, Vol. 41, 2015. https://ssrn.com/abstract=2483728

INDEX

Made in United States
Orlando, FL
11 November 2026

90609403R00118